BeesKnees #1:
A Beekeeping Memoir

Volume One: Days 1 - 100

The Journey of a Beginning Beekeeper

Fran Stewart

BeesKnees #1: A Beekeeping Memoir
Fran Stewart
© 2019

All rights reserved. No part of this book may be used or reproduced in any manner whatsoever without written permission from the author, except by a reviewer who may quote brief passages in a review.

Cover design by Darlene Carter

ISBN: 978-1-951368-00-5

This book was printed in the United States of America.

Published by
My Own Ship Press
PO Box 490153
Lawrenceville GA 30049

myownship@icloud.com
franstewart.com

To beginning beekeepers everywhere

Learn from my mistakes and share in my joys

Books by Fran Stewart

<u>The Biscuit McKee Mystery Series</u>:

Orange as Marmalade
Yellow as Legal Pads
Green as a Garden Hose
Blue as Blue Jeans
Indigo as an Iris
Violet as an Amethyst
Gray as Ashes

Red as a Rooster
Black as Soot
Pink as a Peony
White as Ice

A Slaying Song Tonight

<u>The Scot Shop Mysteries</u>:

A Wee Murder in My Shop
A Wee Dose of Death
A Wee Homicide in the Hotel

Poetry:

Resolution

For Children:

As Orange As Marmalade/
   Tan naranja como Mermelada
        (a bilingual book)

Non-Fiction:

From The Tip of My Pen: a workbook for writers
BeesKnees #1: A Beekeeping Memoir

Introduction

This is the first of six volumes of my bee blog, which was originally e-published on http://beeskneesbeekeeping.blogspot.com. I'd made a commitment to myself, and announced it to a number of friends, that I would blog for 600 days straight. I did it, too, except for one little vacation I had to take when I had surgery after Day #575.

Since going back to the beginning of a blog and scrolling (and scrolling and scrolling) can be a big pain in the tutu, I decided to compile the entries into a more readable format, thereby making life easier for my family, my friends, my fans, and for anyone else who is interesting in learning more about bees.

Altogether the 600 entries represent my journey into, through, and out of the world of beekeeping. If you're considering beekeeping yourself, I'd suggest that you educate yourself ahead of time—but then again, it's your life. Maybe you're the type that likes simply to jump into something.

That's fine, but I hope you'll somehow or other avoid most of the mistakes I made.

I should note that the gorgeously detailed cover photo is from Pexels.com (Pixabay) and all the photos used in the rest of the book are from the public domain unless noted otherwise. Darlene Carter at *Journey of a Dream Press* created the cover designs for all six of these volumes.

I've been teaching a series of classes on how to write memoirs—the stories of your life. A memoir (singular, as opposed to "memoirs" plural) is a story that focuses on only one aspect of a life. These six volumes of my beekeeping blog are just such a memoir.

Here and there I've updated some of the entries. You'll find those changes bracketed and beginning like this: *[2019 Note . . .]* I've also corrected some of the typos that snuck their way into my online entries.

If you want more details about the stories of my life, you'll have to read my memoirs (plural). But I have to publish them first. Don't hold your breath waiting.

In the meantime, I wish you joy.

> --Fran
> from my house beside a creek
> on the other side of Hog Mountain GA
> Summer 2019

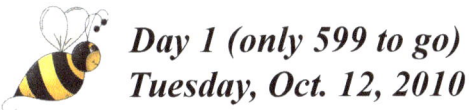
Day 1 (only 599 to go)
Tuesday, Oct. 12, 2010

I never knew there was so much to learn about bees. There seems to be a drastic division within the beekeeping community, with those who advocate the large-cell foundations, which result in larger bees that are more prone to attack by varroa mites (nasty little buggers) on one side, and the so-called "natural beekeepers" on the other. Guess which side I'm on?

I learned about the natural approach through reading *The Complete Idiot's Guide to Beekeeping*. I checked it out from the library, but have ordered a copy from my favorite independent bookstore, Cowan's Book Nook in Blue Ridge GA. I plan to use only the small-cell foundation, so I can have healthier and, I would assume, happier bees.

What's **foundation**, you ask? Well, it's a sheet of very thin beeswax that is stamped in a pattern of hexagonal ridges. When the bees build comb, as they've done for more than 14 million years in the wild, they don't need foundation, but beekeepers find that by giving the bees the foundation to start with, the bees create honeycombs that are more convenient for said beekeepers who want to rob—er, harvest—the honey.

I think I'm going to start with one hive with foundation already in it, and one hive where I give the bees a chance to build their own. Then again, since the only thing I know about bees comes from the fifteen books I've read so far, I may change my mind by day 60 of this blog.

I'll keep you informed every step of the way.

BeeAttitude for day 1: *Blessed are they who use no pesticides, for they shall be healthy - and so shall we bees.*

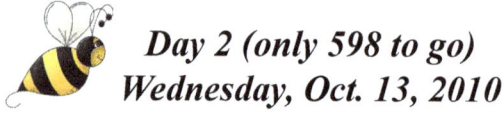
Day 2 (only 598 to go)
Wednesday, Oct. 13, 2010

Well, Day #1 was great fun. Just getting the blog started felt like quite an accomplishment. Almost like the feeling I got when I made pickled beets a week or so ago. What do pickled beets have to do with bees, other than the common first three letters? I'm glad you asked.

You see, bees are incredibly tidy little critters. The worker bees spend their entire life cycle moving in a methodical way from one task, such as cleaning out the brood cells, to feeding the babies and attending the queen, to fanning the honey (that evaporates the excess water and gets the honey down to 18% humidity, which is what keeps the honey from going bad), to working as guards or house bees, and then on to the outside foraging jobs. I may have skipped a job or two, but you get the idea.

Anyway, the house bees are responsible for picking up any garbage and tossing it out the door. If a mouse sneaks in to try to rob the honey, the guard bees sting it to death. The trouble with that is that the house bees can't pick it up and toss it outside. So the bees coat the mouse with propolis (that's a glue-like substance that they make from tree sap). The coating keeps the mouse from rotting and stinking up the hive, rather like mummification, although I must admit I've never smelled a mummy.

But I was talking about beets. I went to the Lawrenceville Farmer's Market a couple of Saturdays ago and picked up, among other things, a big bunch of beets. Had fun introducing them to my grandchildren, who had never tasted raw beet. After that, we cooked one and they ate it with gusto. (I have wonderful, culinarily adventuresome grandchildren.) Over the next few days I ate beets for breakfast (they made the eggs turn pink), lunch (they don't taste great in lasagna), and dinner (pretty good). I'd bought too many beets, though. So I pulled out an old Betty Crocker cookbook that I'd gotten as a wedding present in 1968. And I pickled the remaining beets! That's not exactly like propolizing a dead mouse, but it did prevent the beets from getting slimy.

I'll give you the recipe (for beets, not mouse), just in case you're interested. If you're not, just skip down to the **BeeAttitude** for the day.

Cook a bunch of beets (boil them for a while).
Peel and slice them. Put the skins in your compost pile.
Mix a cup of water, a half-cup of vinegar, a cup of sugar (or substitute agave nectar), and a stick of cinnamon. I didn't have a cinnamon stick, so I just threw in a half-teaspoon of the stuff.
Pour all this over the beets and let them sit overnight in the 'fridge.

Enjoy.

Betty Crocker started with a can of sliced beets. That's no fun at all.

BeeAttitude for Day #2: *Blessed are they who plant bee-friendly flowers, for they shall have music all summer long.*

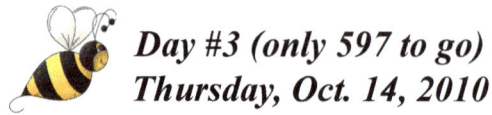
Day #3 (only 597 to go)
Thursday, Oct. 14, 2010

Last night, I couldn't seem to sleep, so I got up and wandered out onto my back deck, where the bees will be installed come springtime. I sat there for quite a while, absorbing the night sounds, full of insect noises and, unfortunately, the rumble from Interstate 85 a mile or so away. Fortunately that sound was somewhat muffled by all the trees behind my house.

Whales used to be able to hear other whales' songs half an ocean away, but now, with all the underwater noise from ships and boats and subs, and the supersonic booms from the air above, the world of the whale has shrunk. Honeybees, though, communicate mostly through smell and movement, so I don't think they're affected so much by our noise pollution. At least not in my backyard.

If you remove a queen bee from her hive, the workers will almost immediately know that they are queen-less, because her uniquely scented pheromones will no longer be present. The workers then will begin forming extra-large queen cells and stuffing them with Royal Jelly, the protein-rich substance that creates a queen bee.

Strange bees that enter a hive are challenged by the guard bees—those strangers don't smell right. Baby bees that have died before emerging smell different than healthy babies, and the nurse bees will empty the cells of the corpses, pass the dead bees to the house bees to toss out of the hive, and clean the cells to make them ready for the queen's next egg-laying pass. Bees smell the pollen and nectar on their incoming hive mates; they smell the consistency of the honey as it is gradually evaporated to the correct consistency.

And then there's the movement. The ways bees dance to communicate is intricate enough to need entire books to explain how they do it. Suffice it to say that a foraging bee can fly home and do a special dance to tell the other bees the quality of a nectar source, where it is (both the direction from the hive and the distance from the hive), and probably a bunch of other things I haven't learned about yet.

    As a writer, I'm a firm proponent of the power of the written word, but I must admit I'm awed by the ways whales and honeybees talk to each other. Wouldn't it be fun to speak their language?

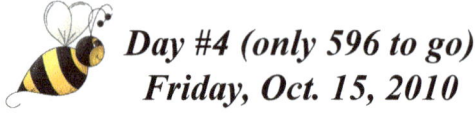
Day #4 (only 596 to go)
Friday, Oct. 15, 2010

I attended a meeting of the Gwinnett Beekeepers Club last Tuesday. Since there were so many of us there who had never kept bees, the leaders went through ALL the equipment needed for a beekeeping operation. This is, of course, assuming that one wants to harvest honey. The equipment is for the convenience of the keeper. It is not a necessity for the bees. After all, those critters have been around since before the dinosaurs. We know that because a honeybee, trapped in amber 14 million years ago, recently came to light.

So, they don't really need us, but we sure need them. Think of every fruit or veggie you've eaten in the past twelve months. Not the grains—wheat and oats and such are pollinated by the wind. The fruit trees and gardens, though, whether huge commercial operations or small back yard plots, need bees. NO BEES translates to no food for us. I sure don't want to live exclusively on oatmeal and rice and whole wheat bread.

Hillside Rice Paddy © Yelloideas Photography

The equipment, though. My gosh! I could spend a fortune on this endeavor. Of course, there are ways to cut corners. Instead of spending $63 on a huge white bee suit with built-in elastic straps to seal my pant legs and wrists (so bees won't crawl in there to investigate), I went to Goodwill and spent $8 on some oversized white pants and long-sleeved shirts. I figure two layers of each with something like Velcro straps around my wrists and with my socks pulled up over the pant legs will do me just fine. I am NOT going to post a picture of me wearing them, but I figure the bees won't care how silly I look.

Why are beekeeping suits always white? Bees get really curious about dark colors. So if you visit a hive, wear light-colored clothes.

I will invest in a bee veil—don't want to get stung on my face or neck in case I do something dumb to upset the bees. You see, honeybees are very gentle. Unless they feel threatened, in which case it is their duty to protect the hive. They will literally give their lives to protect the hive and the queen. If a worker bee stings, she dies. So, a $35 bee veil is a good investment. Cheaper ones (that still work well) are half that price. I just saved $17!

And a smoker. This is a fat can with a tube-shaped exhaust at the top and a bellows attached on the side. You start some newspaper burning in it, stuff in a bunch of pine needles or other such fuel, close it up, pump on the bellows, and smoke will drift out of the tube. Smoking the bees will calm them. At the meeting we were advised to buy a smoker right away and practice, practice, practice, so that when the time came to calm a suspicious hive, we wouldn't have our smoker go out at the wrong time. $36 for a good basic smoker. Should last for years.

Four dollars will buy me an Italian hive tool and another four for a bee brush. One helps open a hive that's stuck shut with propolis, and the other is for gently brushing bees off a comb when I need to take it away from them.

$22 for a frame holder, a metal doohickey that I can hook over the side of the hive body so that, as I lift out frames to inspect them, I don't have to set them on the ground and risk squashing bees, stepping on the comb, or getting grass or dirt stuck to the foundation.

Gloves are a good idea, and there are styles that range up to $17, but one of the books I read suggested getting some yellow rubber gloves from the household department at the grocery store. They work just fine. Eventually, the goal is to get to where you're comfortable not wearing gloves at all. If you get stung—refer back to the hive tool. It's good for scraping out the stinger.

I'm up to $143 so far (if I added correctly), and I still don't have the wooden hives or the bees. I'll worry about that later. After all, this is only Day #4.

BeeAttitude for Day #4: *Blessed are they who wear light-colored clothes, for we shall not pay any attention to them.*

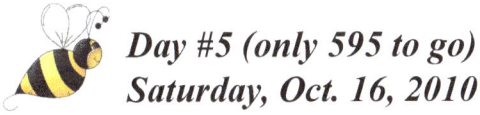 *Day #5 (only 595 to go)*
Saturday, Oct. 16, 2010

My sister called me several days ago and asked, "Did you know that Granddaddy kept bees?" Well, no; I hadn't known that. It seems my grandfather, who was a Mississippi farmer all his life, used to have beehives. He kept them for years, never used any protective equipment, and—we would guess—got plenty of honey from them.

Then, one day, my sister told me, he got badly stung, had a severe allergic reaction, and got rid of his hives, never again to keep bees.

The trouble with third-hand stories like this is that one can't get details. My grandfather died years ago. And my dad has been gone for eight years. I never thought to ask him about his father's role as a beekeeper, because I didn't know to ask. Was he really stung by the bees, or did he perhaps stumble on a yellow-jacket nest? I'll never know.

What other stories have I lost along the way, simply because I didn't know what to ask about? What are the stories that *you* haven't heard - or haven't told anyone?

It's time to start writing down our stories, so that grandchildren, nieces, nephews, siblings, children, will have a way of connecting when we're not around to answer the questions. I have copies of my grandfather's diaries. I can't recall ever having seen a reference to bees. But then again, I wasn't looking for that when I read through them.

Time to go back and read them with a specific topic in mind. There's no telling what I'll find.

BeeAttitude for Day #5: *Blessed are they who keep their hands in their pockets when visiting us, for they shall not frighten us with flailing arms.*

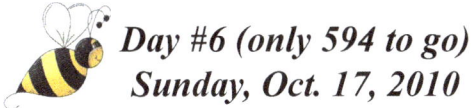 Day #6 (only 594 to go)
Sunday, Oct. 17, 2010

To bee or not to bee . . . that is sort of the question.

I'm pretty sure I'm not dreadfully allergic to bee venom, but there's a niggly little question in my gut about it. What if I put all this work into setting up a hive and then find out I swell up like a pumpkin when I get stung? It really would bee (sorry) better to find out ahead of time, don't you think?

So, I'm going to find an allergist who can test me. I'll let you know how much it costs so you can add it to the list I made a few blog posts ago.

This is a short one. It's 11:11 p.m. as I write this. I've been at a reception that was great fun - harp music, poetry readings, and lots of great conversation, but now everything's cleaned up, the guests are all gone, and I'm kinda pooped. So good night. This post is scheduled to go out into the world at 12:01 a.m. That's because I can never remember if midnight is supposed to be AM or PM. Ditto with noon. Bees don't worry about stuff like that. They're sound asleep at 11:11 p.m.

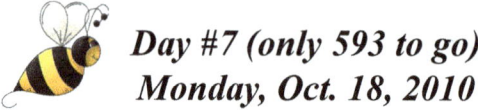
Day #7 (only 593 to go)
Monday, Oct. 18, 2010

Have I mentioned yet that I gave up sugar a few weeks ago? It was working just fine until I attended a Board meeting in a gracious old house -- and there were bowls of candy corn here and there around the place. So much for my resolution.

Bees don't have that problem. A honeybee would never say, "Gee, I'm tired of being a vegetarian. I think I'll try to eat a cow." Humans are omnivores. That's what gets us into trouble. Because we can eat such a wide range of foods - and because our bodies seem to need that wide range - we lay ourselves open to temptation on every side.

Bees have been gathering nectar and pollen for millions of years, and they've done just fine with that standard diet. They feed their babies honey and pollen and Royal Jelly. And water. That's it. Sounds very uncomplicated, doesn't it?

Well, I'm in a mood right now that has me thinking that simplicity is a particularly good idea. Maybe it's all the sugar I've been ingesting. Sugar makes me grumpy, and I don't like that. Maybe I should go watch a bee for a while—if I could find one. How long till Spring, when I can have bees right here on my back deck?

BeeAttitude for Day #6: *Blessed are they who eat local honey, for they shall be healthier as a result.*

Day #8 Just a spoonful of honey
Tuesday, Oct. 19, 2010

If you approach a honeybee hive on a warm morning, you're liable to see a whole bunch of bees flying in circles around it. These bees are memorizing what the hive looks like from many different angles. They fly fairly close to it, then in ever widening circles, just like Rilke, who said he lived his life that way. By studying the hive in relation to the landmarks around it - a tree, a large shrub, a shed, the corner of the garage - they lessen the chance of their getting lost when they go out on their foraging flights.

Those flights, during which they collect the nectar and pollen that supports the hive through the winter, are the last of the jobs they perform for the hive. In its entire life cycle, a single honeybee produces one-twelfth of a teaspoon of honey. That's right. It takes a dozen bees to create the spoonful of honey you put in your tea this morning.

Let's hear it for the honeybees!

592 days to go in this journey. Wonder if I'll make it?

BeeAttitude for Day #8 *Blessed are they who appreciate bees, for they are a blessing to us.*

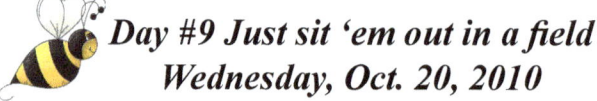 *Day #9 Just sit 'em out in a field*
Wednesday, Oct. 20, 2010

This afternoon I rode on MARTA back from the Atlanta airport, and I got to talking about beekeeping with someone who sat down near me. A young soldier sitting in the next seat spoke up and said his parents kept bees, and that he'd been around them since he was two years old.

"All you need to do ma'am, is just sit 'em out in a field and watch them. There's not an awful lot to it."

Well, that's my thought, pretty much, too. I do want to be a bit more involved, though, which is why I'm spending all this time reading about bees and beekeeping.

Tomorrow, after I get back from my dentist appointment, I'm going to plant some red clover seed on the side of my front yard. I bought it through Gwinnett Locally Grown at Rancho Alegre, a nearby organic farm. Hopefully it will bloom next year just in time for me to sit in a nearby chair and watch the bees collecting nectar for clover honey. Gotta figure out how to call the rain so the clover will germinate . . .

Rice Paddy Before the Rice © Yelloideas Photography

NO! ! ! I don't want this much rain ! ! ! Hmm . . . Any good ideas on how to prevent that?

BeeAttitude for Day #9: *Blessed are the "natural" beekeepers, for their honey shall be pure and their bees shall be happy and healthy.*

Day #10 - 3,500 Bees per Pound
Thursday, Oct. 21, 2010

Fun Facts about Bees: (I pulled these tidbits from *The Beekeeper's Handbook* by Diana Sammataro & Alphonse Avitabile.)

A "fully-loaded" bee flies 6 to 9 miles per hour
When a bee is "empty," she lazes along at 8 mph
Bees can fly up to eight miles from their hive, but they usually stay within a 2-mile radius

Nectar Collecting:
- 100-1,500 flowers per load
- up to 29 round trips per day
- a trip can last from 5 to 150 minutes

In order to produce 150 pounds of honey, the bees in one hive have to fly the equivalent of 13 trips to the moon and back again.

I have 590 more days to go on my blog. I wonder, in terms of effort, how that compares to even one trip to the moon. Bees are amazing, aren't they?

BeeAttitude for Day #10: *Blessed are they who care enough about us to learn what we need, for they shall be full of interesting facts to astound their friends.*

 ### *Day #11 Could I Carry 115 pounds?*
Friday, Oct. 22, 2010

I just read that a bee can carry 85% of its body weight when it's fully loaded with nectar.

My gosh! I'd have to carry **114.75 pounds** to do that kind of work. *Okay - go ahead and do the math.*

Not only that, but I'd have to carry it up to 29 trips per day. Do bees get coffee breaks?

Actually, they do get breaks. They fly into the hive and sit there for a short while, resting; but then they're right out the door again. Feisty little critters, aren't they?

BeeAttitude for Day #11: *Blessed are they who keep bees, for their gardens (and those of their neighbors) shall be pollinated.*

 ## *Day #12 Handmade Soaps and Beeswax*
Saturday, Oct. 23, 2010

While I was in Washington DC last week, I went to the DuPont Circle Farmer's Market on Sunday morning. What a great collection of people who care about the environment. I wandered from stall to stall, talking to everybody. Met some beekeepers, knitters, soap makers. You name it, there was someone selling it.

The soap I bought is made from an olive oil base. It's probably just as well it doesn't contain beeswax. It's very hard to buy beeswax that isn't polluted with some amount of toxins, since beekeepers for so long have medicated their bees, and the meds pass right into the wax the bees excrete. *Not from that end! The wax comes from special glands on the front of their tummies.*

I think I'll be okay once I actually have my bees. They don't like smelly stuff like hairsprays (neither do I) or heavy perfumes, but the soap fragrance is light and wonderful. I'll let you know next spring what the bees think of it.

BeeAttitude for Day #12: *Blessed are they who come to us not wearing perfumes or hair spray, for they shall not confuse us.*

Day #13 I'm wondering if I can stand it
Sunday, Oct. 24, 2010

If you're looking for a funny blog this morning, this one won't be it. Come back tomorrow, when I promise I'll be brighter.

Last year, between the end of October and the middle of December, I had to have three of my beloved older cats put down. Waldo had battled kidney disorders for several years; Harley developed an enormous brain tumor; and Jazzminka had squamous cell carcinoma.

All my cats have been rescues, but often I felt that they were the ones who had rescued me. Jazzminka cured my thyroid, for instance. I'd given them all a good indoor life, with as much affection, brushing, and holding as they wanted. Twelve years ago Waldo wandered into my garage bleeding and starving, and never wanted to go outside again as long as he lived. I could leave a door open, and he wouldn't approach it. They had plenty of exercise, for they all loved to run up and down the cat trees and ramps that grace my house. But then, one day, for each of them, it was time to let go.

At beekeepers meetings, I've heard of people who've lost entire hives. There are so many ways in which honeybees can be threatened. The fact that bees have, as a species, survived for countless years (a lot longer than the dinosaurs lasted), still does not guarantee that the hives I'm planning for my back deck will make it.

As with my cats, I can give them as much nurturing as I'm able, and something still may happen that will doom the hive. Right now, I'm wondering if I can stand it. At least with my cats, I was able to hold each of them as they made their transition across the rainbow bridge. But it's hard to hold a bee.

Worker bees in the summer have a life span of five or six weeks. But a hive, the social unit of the bee, can last for years and years. Until pesticides or inept beekeepers get in the way.

I'm going to go make myself a cup of tea and sit in my rocking chair, where Miss Polly or Daisy will find my lap. Purrs help combat sadness. So do sunrises and writing and farmer's markets and singing and reading and having lunch with friends and . . .

Maybe I'm not so sad after all.

BeeAttitude for Day #13: *Blessed are they who love without reservation, for they shall have full hearts.*

 Day #14 Ever seen a corbicula? Monday, Oct. 25, 2010

Okay - I'm better today. No more sniffing in my tea.

photo credit: Veronica Lowe

Do you know what a **corbicula** is? Neither did I until a few minutes ago when I read it in *The Beekeeper's Handbook*. I think I've read about it before this, but it only this minute sank in. A corbicula is a pollen collecting "basket" shaped like a flattened depression surrounded by curved spines of the outside of a bee's hind legs. Worker bees have two of them, one on each back leg. When they're fully loaded with pollen, the bee looks like it's toting a pair of cute little yellow saddlebags.

I looked for a photo of a corbicula, but the closest I could find was a butterfly bush with a yellow butterfly (in my daughter's yard).

I can't wait to see my honeybees all yellowed up. Only six more months until I get the bees. Then, who knows how long it will "bee" until I see the corbiculae filled with golden particles. Reading about it sets up some glorious anticipation. Temple Grandin, in her book *Animals in*

Translation says that anticipation is often more satisfying than the end result. I saw the movie *Temple Grandin* and was so impressed I'm reading her books. So far, though, she hasn't said anything about bees.

BeeAttitude for Day #14: *Blessed are they who respect us for who we are and what we do, for they shall be satisfied with their lives.*

Day #15 More Fun Bee Facts
Tuesday, Oct. 26, 2010

I used to think I worked hard at caring for my children when they were babies. All those wide-awake nights, all those feedings, all those diapers (cloth, not disposable!), all those little hand-sewn outfits . . .

Well, I don't know what dinosaurs had to go through to rear their babies, but we humans have an easy job compared to bees. Before the queen bee can lay an egg, 25 to 30 bees work about 41 minutes to prepare the cell for her. Then, once the egg has become a larva, 1,300 bees visit it, doing baby-tending stuff. In fact, each larva will get 7,200 bee visits during its stay in the cell. Once it hatches, 60 bees work at cleaning the cell to ready it for the next egg.

Once again, I took these facts from *The Beekeeper's Handbook*, which was loaned to me by an experienced beekeeper who belongs to the Gwinnett Beekeepers Club. Beekeepers are generous people, willing to share their expertise. I'm going to have to get my own copy of that book, though, so he can loan his copy to somebody else.

One more fact: One bee can collect anywhere from 250,000 to 600,000 grains of pollen at a time. I keep being amazed by these little critters.

BeeAttitude for Day #15: *Blessed are they who advise brand new beekeepers, for they shall help us bees get better treatment.*

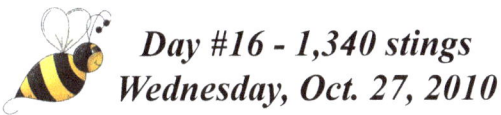 Day #16 - 1,340 stings
Wednesday, Oct. 27, 2010

Well, this is good. I just read that a lethal dose of venom would come from getting ten stings for every pound of body weight. For me, that means 1,340 stings. Guess I'm safe, because I just can't imagine that I'll make that many bees feel threatened.

On a happier note, bees beat their wings at a rate that's about halfway between mosquitos and grasshoppers. Aren't you glad to know that? I'm just glad that bees don't whine like mosquitos. I think that would drive me nuts. Instead, I'm looking forward to lazy mornings sitting on the deck listening to the hum of the bees as they work while I sip tea and write. The cats can look out the window, if they'll get out of their paper bags first.

Panther in a bag

Life is good.

BeeAttitude for Day #16: *Blessed are they who respect all animals, for they shall be more aware of what we can teach them.*

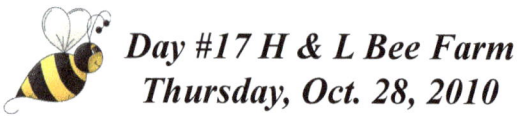

Day #17 H & L Bee Farm
Thursday, Oct. 28, 2010

Today (Wednesday) I drove four hours (one way) to check out the H & L Bee Farm in Ocilla, GA, and five hours back (there were accidents on I-285). It was well worth the trip!

[2019 Note: As you will learn later, I withdraw any recommendations I might have made about H&L. Beware those first impressions. I was so caught up in my excitement about getting bees—and I was so ignorant about what I should be looking for—I bought the hives and later the bees without enough research.]

Not only did I see the hives up close as Brenda drove me around the Bee Farm on an electric cart, I came home with my very own **Deluxe Garden Hive** in **Rubber Duck Yellow.** If I could figure out how to do it, I'd show you a picture of it. I'll have to ask my granddaughter to teach me how to transfer a picture from my phone to my computer.

Now, at 7:30 on Wednesday evening, the hive is sitting in my dining room, with a cat perched on top of it. I haven't put it out on the deck yet because it's pouring, and I don't want the wood to weather any more than necessary. It will be fresh and ready to go **when I get the bees in late March or early April.**

I've already ordered them and put down a deposit. I'll be getting a **nuc** and a **package**. Don't know what those are? You just wait. I'll explain it all in a later post.

The folks at H&L gave me a CD called "Getting Started with Bees." Terry Hester, one of the owners of H & L said it wasn't a Hollywood production. Nope! But it's full of downright helpful information, and now I've seen how to light a smoker, how to place a package of bees in my hive, how to inspect the hives, and so much more.

Meanwhile:

[I know, this is a book, not a hive, but the color is right]

BeeAttitude for Day #17: *Blessed are those who put bands around their wrists and ankles, for we shall not get caught in their clothing and they shall not get stung, so we shall go on to live and produce more honey.*

 ## Day #18 Cinnamon and Honey
Friday, Oct. 29, 2010

Did you know that honey is the only food on the planet that will not spoil or rot? Or so I've heard. If you put it in the 'fridge, it will *crystallize,* but it's still honey and still edible. I put it in my tea that way, and it works just fine. If you want to liquefy it, though, just loosen the lid and sit the honey in a container of hot water. It will melt and be as good as it ever was. **Never boil honey or put it in a microwave.** If you do, you'll kill the enzymes in the honey.

Now, if you combine wonderful Honey with wonderful Cinnamon:

Some people claim that a mixture of honey and cinnamon can cure most diseases. I'm not sure I'd go quite that far, but I do know from my own experience that honey has been a very effective medicine for some of what ails me. Honey can probably be used without any side effects - but that's just a guess on my part.

I found a list that was printed years ago in a crackpot tabloid. The Weekly World News went out of business in 2007, with very good cause - wait till you see the sorts of things they reported.

Its list of what honey and cinnamon could cure included arthritis, bad breath, bladder infections, cancer, cholesterol, colds, fatigue, hearing loss, heart disease, immune system, indigestion, influenza, longevity, skin infections, upset stomach, weight loss. (Forgive the poor syntax in the list. I didn't write it! *Why ever would one want to cure longevity? Or one's immune system?)*

Here's one of their instructions, quoted directly:
<u>HEART DISEASES</u>: Make a paste of honey and cinnamon powder, apply on bread, instead of jelly and jam, and eat it regularly for breakfast. It reduces the cholesterol in the arteries and saves the patient from heart attack. Also, those who have already had an attack, if they do this process daily, they are kept miles away from the next attack. Regular use of the above process relieves loss of breath and strengthens the heart

beat. In America and Canada, various nursing homes have treated patients successfully and have found that as you age, the arteries and veins lose their flexibility and get clogged; honey and cinnamon revitalize the arteries and veins.

Here's another one:
<u>ARTHRITIS</u>: Arthritis patients may take daily, morning and night, one cup of hot water with two spoons of honey and one small teaspoon of cinnamon powder. If taken regularly even chronic arthritis can be cured. In a recent research conducted at the Copenhagen University, it was found that when the doctors treated their patients with a mixture of one tablespoon Honey and half teaspoon Cinnamon powder before breakfast, they found that within a week, out of the 200 people so treated, practically 73 patients were totally relieved of pain, and within a month, mostly all the patients who could not walk or move around because of arthritis started walking without pain.

See why they went out of business? Don't you love the "practically 73 patients"? Does that mean 72 patients? The world needs more editors!

Well, let me know if you try honey/cinnamon and have miraculous results.

©*Yelloideas Photography*

Still, honey and cinnamon both have a lot going for them. I wonder if the two of them together are more effective than each one alone would be - sort of like a good marriage, a respectful partnership, a clown fish and an anemone, or a well-functioning beehive.

I figure it can't hurt - and it might help - so I'm headed to the kitchen to spread some honey and cinnamon on a slice of the homemade bread that a thoughtful neighbor gave me. Yum! It's guaranteed to cure my snack urge.

I'll eat it while I'm looking at my bright yellow hive and planning which perennials I need to plant this fall.

BeeAttitude for Day #18: *Blessed are they who write the truth. We bees don't care, but we know that humans will respect such people.*

Day #19 BEEcoming a Better Human
Saturday, Oct. 30, 2010

Here in Georgia, it's getting to be autumn and the seed pods on my *Aesclepias* (better known as Butterfly Weed) are just about all blown away. My son photographed this milkweed pod several years ago. The picture expresses the wonder I feel when I look at my yard gradually folding into its winter rest. I hope it's getting ready for the bees that will join us in late March or early April.

©Yelloideas Photography

I know this is a blog about beekeeping, but if you get a chance to read *Animals Make Us Human* by Temple Grandin, let me know if you're as impressed with her work as I am. Based on her observations of other animals, I plan to be a lot more careful about the ways in which I look at my bees. I'd like to use the lessons I learn from them to become more fully (good) human myself.

BeeAttitude for Day #19: *Blessed are they who watch us without judgment, for they shall learn great wisdom.*

Something for Which I'm Grateful:
Brown leaves in the dappled sunshine against a bright blue sky

 Day #20 Scary Scary Halloween
Sunday, Oct. 31, 2010

Halloween? Oh, witches and goblins and pirates and princesses and honeybees and . . .

Honeybees? Well, come to think of it, wouldn't that make a cute costume? Imagine a striped costume with wings, toting along a big orange flower:

Yeah, like that.

Or maybe like this... That's close enough to a bee costume, isn't it?

BeesKnees #1: A Beekeeping Memoir

Eli spinning fire

Oooh! Now there's something scary!

BEE safe on Halloween!

BeeAttitude for Day #20: *Blessed are they who eat honey instead of sugar, for they shall have healthy metabolisms.*

Today I am Grateful for: My son, and his amazingly detailed photos - and his fire-spinning, which always astonishes me.

 ### *Day #21 Answer this Bee Joke*
Monday, Nov. 1, 2010

November? I never quite got used to February, and here it is the eleventh month already.

This time of year, beekeepers are usually feeding their bees sugar water. Does this have roughly the same effect as all the Halloween treats on human youngsters? I'd love it if I could have bees that gathered nectar most of the year and went into winter with plenty of honey and pollen stores made from abundant nectar plants.

JOKE TIME: How can you tell if a bee is hyper? (Send your answers to me and I'll announce them in one of my upcoming blogs.)

BeeAttitude for Day #21: *Blessed are they who avoid excess sugar, for they shall BEE calm.*

Today I am grateful for: Public Domain Photos that allow me to show you bees in their natural beauty:

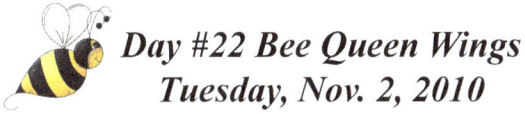

Day #22 Bee Queen Wings
Tuesday, Nov. 2, 2010

It's relatively (if you're an experienced beekeeper) easy to spot the queen. She's the one with the short wings. Not really. They're the same size as the wings of the workers, but her abdomen is a great deal longer than theirs, so her wings just *look* shorter.

Her first few flights allow her to orient herself to the hive so she can find her way back to it. Then she takes off to the drone-gathering place. Don't ask me how she knows where that is - it probably has something to do with smell, but nobody seems to know for sure. After she's mated and returned to the hive, the workers start feeding her lots of good bee food, and her abdomen increases greatly in size. As well it should, since she's going to be laying anywhere up to 2,500 eggs a day for the rest of the season, and for two, three, or even four years after that.

She'll never use her wings for much, unless the hive has to swarm. If the workers decide to leave the hive (because of overcrowding), they stop feeding her as much, so she'll slim down to a weight where her wings can support her. When she's slender enough, half the worker bees in the hive leave, enticing her along in some magical unknown bee language. They all go find another place to live, and the remaining workers get busy on the queen cells they've built up around some regular old eggs. By stuffing those cells with Royal Jelly, they actually *create* a new queen.

And you thought the queen was in charge???? Nope!

BeeAttitude for Day #22: *Blessed are those who tread the ground lightly, for they shall not hurt our food sources.*

One thing I'm grateful for right now: *Smiles and hugs from my grandchildren.*

# Day #23 Scents and Scentsibility
Wednesday, Nov. 3, 2010

For reasons I'll explain later, as I was writing yesterday, I meant to type the word *centimeter*, but it came out *sentimeter*. Before I corrected it, I connected it to *sentiment*. As I played around with the words (writers do that sort of thing) I came up with:

- **Scentimeter:** what a worker bee uses to distinguish her hive mates from outsiders
- **Scentillate:** the action of making bees curious by wearing a particular perfume
- **Scentiment:** the warm feeling I get when I recall my dad's *Old Spice* aftershave, hoping the bees would have liked it if they could have met him
- **Scentient:** really, really smart about figuring things out by using what they smell like
- **Scentsibility:** what inspired Jane Austen to write as she sat among the beehives in her family's garden.

Did Jane Austen have beehives? I don't know. I can't recall her mentioning bees in any of her books, but I'm sure there are Austen devotees who could set me straight.

That's enough for now. If you come up with any other **scent**sible words, put your two-scents worth in a comment, message, or email!

<u>Good news</u>: Yesterday I took out my little plastic ruler with the inches on one side and the centimeters (see? I told you I'd explain my thought processes!) on the other. I measured the itty bitty hexagonal ridges on the wax foundation and found that they are indeed SMALL cell (as opposed to STANDARD size). That means I'll have a better shot at raising healthy bees who can naturally oppose the various mites and beetles that attack the larger honeybees raised by large honey-sellers.

Incidentally, STANDARD in this case means what the large corporate manufacturers and beekeepers have decided to sell and use, so they can push the bees into growing bigger and storing more easily extracted honey. The bees had nothing to say about it. The *bee standard* is *small*.

BeeAttitude for Day #23: *Blessed are those who train their noses, for they shall avoid unpleasant surprises.*

One thing I am grateful for: *My various grandchildren, who delighted me and scared me silly with their Halloween costumes of ladybug, pirate, and ghouls, and who also shared some of their candy with me.*

Contributions from readers:
Scentsitive – The condition of a bee's antennae
Scentsitize – How beekeepers get used to being stung occasionally
Scentsible – What people are when they refuse to use pesticides

Day #24 We Have a Winner
Thursday, Nov. 4, 2010

Three days ago I asked you, "How can you tell if a bee is hyper?"

The winning answer came from Pete Ogg in Houston:

"You can tell a bee is hyper if she breaks out in hives!"

Petie emailed me with the answer and said that it's rainy in her part of Houston. She's been a regular follower of the BeesKnees blog since it started.

I'll probably come up with another question at some point. If you think of a good bee joke, though, email me and I'll put it in the blog.

BeeAttitude for Day #24: *Blessed are they who laugh, for they shall experience the sweetness of life.*

One thing I'm grateful for right now: *The guy from E-Z Out Tree Service who, later on today, is going to take out the tree that fell across my power line. Wish him safety and speediness, please!*

 ## Day #25 Do you ever thank your poll workers?
Friday, Nov. 5, 2010

"Busy as a bee" took on a new meaning last Tuesday, when I volunteered as an elections official. This is the third election I've worked. In the same way that most people don't know what goes on inside a beehive, I think most people never think about what it takes to facilitate an election.

Each election starts (for the poll worker) several months in advance. The person who is in charge of the precinct has to get her team together, and then be sure that they're trained properly. In my case, Juanita (our precinct leader) let me know when the special training sessions were held. Then it was up to me to attend one. I had to reschedule my chiropractic appointment so I could attend on a Friday morning. I had to go Friday because I was scheduled for a book signing on that particular Saturday.

Then there was the online training, which took several hours. We had to pass a test after we went through the training in order to be eligible to work the polls. Whew!

The Monday evening before an election, all the poll workers congregate at the precinct to set up the voting machines, be sure all the crates and boxes and files and folders are present and accounted for, and arrange the tables in a way that makes the flow of traffic simple and easy to understand. Sometimes this works better than other times. This year, for instance, we received a "suggested layout" from the elections office. The end result was that when voters began to bunch up, as happened quite often on Tuesday, I got to play traffic-coordinator. I felt like the scarecrow in the Wizard of Oz. *You can go this way, or you can go that way...*

Monday night, we all set our alarm clocks *(*The instructions suggest we *"set two so you'll be sure to get up on time!"*) at a ridiculously early hour. Tuesday we have to be in the precinct by six o'clock so we can be sworn in *(raise your right hand...),* post all the outside signs, and set up all the last-minute equipment. Then, we have to stay there until everything is packed up at the end of the day. In our case it was nine p.m. We had a running competition going as to how many voters our precinct would process in the twelve-hour period. About ten a.m. I guessed we'd have 1,141. The final tally was 1,146. Yeah! I won!

Sitting in a molded plastic school chair or standing on a gym floor (there are no other choices) for fourteen hours gives job security to chiropractors. The good news, though, was that even though we stayed busy as the proverbial bees all day long, we also got a chance to say hello to some of the most responsible people in this nation - those who choose to vote. And don't get me wrong. We DID get breaks - so we could go stand in the linoleum-floored break room and eat from the great potluck goodies that we all brought in.

Today, my feet are still as sore as a bee's wings. I think. When I get my bees in the spring, I'll have to ask them how they feel after a long hard day of foraging.

BeeAttitude for Day #25: *Blessed are those who vote, for they shall have the right to complain.*

One thing I'm grateful for right now: *The one and only person last Tuesday who said, "Thank you for working here at the polls."*

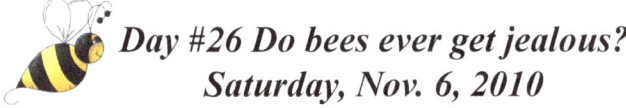 Day #26 Do bees ever get jealous?
Saturday, Nov. 6, 2010

I do wonder sometimes whether jealousy is a strictly human emotion. I've never heard of a jealous bee.

Now, bees *are* territorial. They protect their hives. A wasp who wanders into a beehive is going to be in trouble. And a newly hatched queen bee will do her darndest to kill off the as-yet-unhatched competition queens. But I've been reading lately about ways to **combine hives**, because the more bees a hive has, the more likely it is to make it through the winter. "More bees" means "more workers," which translates into "more honey and pollen stores."

I'm going to have to learn a lot more before I ever try it – heck, I have to get my bees first, which is still five months away – but once I have them, how will I know whether a hive is weak, whether a queen needs to be replaced, whether there is enough honey for them to survive the cold weather?

I think I'm going to need a lot of encouragement when it comes time to harvest my first batch of honey. What if I take too much?

Oh quit it, Frannie. People have been harvesting honey (that's a euphemism - it really amounts to robbing hives) for a kazillion years, and there are plenty of books and articles and even YouTube videos about how to do it. All it takes is a bee veil, a bucket, a warm knife, and a whole lot of courage. I'm not afraid of the bees. I'm afraid of my lack of expertise.

To get back to the jealousy idea though, when I look at videos of all those thousands of bees in a hive, each one going about her work, each one intent on doing what needs to be done, I think there isn't room for anything as petty as jealousy. Of course, bees aren't impressed by designer shoes or stock portfolios, which probably goes a long way to explain the difference between bees and us.

BeeAttitude for Day #26: *Blessed are those who do what needs to be done, for they shall thrive.*

One thing I'm grateful for right now: *The rain that is helping to sprout the red clover I planted for the bees.*

 Day #27 My azaleas will have a new life
Sunday, Nov. 7, 2010

Well, my handy man came by today (Saturday) to dig up the azalea roots that had stymied me. If you'll remember, I cut them down to prevent my bees from gorging themselves on toxic azalea nectar, but I was left with huge masses of thoroughly entrenched roots that my poor shovel and I couldn't get anywhere with. So, my handy-dandy handyman, whose business is called *All Things New,* came with his son and dug them up for me.

I figure that was quite a sacrifice. Look what I lost:

I tended to be happy when I was sitting beside the azaleas in the spring. I even color-coded my turtleneck to match them:

But Mark is taking them home to plant in his yard. They get a new life! I'm not a murderer! His yard is, he assures me, farther than five miles from my house, so I won't have to worry about my bees eating these azaleas or any of the others that, according to him, cover his yard from one end to the other.

Not that many of my neighbors have azaleas, either. In fact, in the spring, my yard has always been the one really bright spot in the neighborhood. What on earth am I going to plant that can take their place? If you have any ideas, I'd appreciate them! They have to be plants that thrive in Georgia, though.

BeeAttitude for Day #27: *Blessed are they who save plants (even if we bees shouldn't eat them), for they shall live surrounded by beauty.*

More than one thing I'm grateful for right now: *The men who cut down my dead trees Friday, the inside plumber who installed a new (NON-LEAKING!) toilet Friday, the outside plumber who will come on Monday to replace the old blue line from my water meter to the inside of my house, my son who helped me shred up a driveway full of dead azalea branches Friday. People (not things) are what matter.*

 ## Day #28 Grannie's Bee Lessons
Monday, Nov. 8, 2010

My grandkids came to visit Friday night while their mother was at an awards dinner for The Hope Clinic in Lawrenceville. We had great fun. We **ate** stove toast (I don't have a toaster, so I toast bread by buttering the slices and frying them in a sauté pan until they're golden brown - the kids think it's gourmet fare. They drew monster pictures and fancy designs. We heated up some soup and **ate** it. They told jokes. We made butter from some extra creamy goat's milk, and **ate** it on crackers. We **baked** Grannie's special Molasses Chewy Cookies, and then we **ate** some of them.

For somebody who's never liked to cook, I sure do a lot of it around my grandkids.

Anyway after the cookies, they asked me about the yellow four-tiered hive I have sitting in my dining room. So I took it apart and explained all the pieces. Then the questions came about how the bees operate, how they find the flowers to pollinate, why there's only one queen per hive, why to use a **queen excluder** (one of the parts of the hive), and how bees find their way home if they fly five miles away from the hive.

We talked about bees for about two hours. For a fifth-grader and a second-grader, that's a long attention span. Then it was time for them to leave. I sent them home with some cookies in a bag.

Day #29 My new end table
Tuesday, Nov. 9, 2010

Imagine this:

Rubber Duck Yellow Hive

Imagine it sitting in my dining area **where I have to walk around it** every time I want to go to the kitchen.

Now imagine it **sitting in my living room** as an end table. Much better, eh? It will have to sit there only until late March or early April, when the bees arrive.

What did I do with the previous end table? I'm taking it to Goodwill tomorrow.

What will I do when I lose this end table? Buy another hive - maybe a blue one, so I'll be ready when my bees outgrow the yellow hive.

BeeAttitude for Day #29: *Blessed are they who can laugh at their furniture, for they shall not be tied to meaningless things.*

One thing I'm grateful for right now: *The new gate on my back deck.*

 ## Day #30 Digging under the driveway
Wednesday, Nov. 10, 2010

When Brant Keiser from **Keep Smiling Plumbing** came here to replace a dead toilet last Friday, he noticed that my house, built in 1985, still had the old brittle horrible blue poly pipe running from the water main to the inside of the house. He saw it because he was down in the crawl space checking out my water heater that hadn't been working well. He recommended Jeff Guinn who owns **Bulldog Plumbing**. Brant does plumbing *inside* houses. Jeff works *outside*. Anyway, Jeff came over right away and gave me an estimate for replacing the blue stuff. He came back Monday to dig under the driveway and down to the front of my house, bore a hole through my foundation, and connect the new pipe. Whew! I'm happy to say it all went well, especially considering the fact that on Monday, just before Jeff got here, the outside pipe sprung a leak. If all this flap hadn't happened, I'd be swimming in a sea of mud.

Blue poly has a life expectancy of 7 to 14 years. Mine lasted 25. Hallelujah!

The other good news is that I had an opportunity to clean out a lot of the stuff in my garage (Goodwill, here I come!) to make room for the new water heater. Brant said a water heater had no business being in a crawl space. I trust my plumber, and I'm glad he's the one toting toilets and water heaters around, so I don't have to learn how to do it.

Speaking of heavy equipment, on the toilet day, Friday, I had three trees removed. One had fallen across my power line; one had obviously already been dying since most of its leaves fell off in June, and the third one was leaning precariously over my roof. **E-Z Out Tree Service** did a great job. The logs that remain, because I asked for them, have a gorgeous sunburst pattern of dead wood in the center of each of them.

With my new cell phone, I took some pictures of the wood, but now I can't figure out how to get the photos out of my camera and into my computer. My granddaughter says I can't email them to myself because

I don't pay extra to have text messaging capability. And I don't have a little USB doohickie. **Technology makes our lives a whole lot easier – except when I don't know how to use it.**

What does this have to do with bees? Well, it makes me glad I don't have the bees yet, because I'd hate to think of any of them being run over by the heavy equipment the workers had to use. I know, that's stretching it a bit, to make a connection like that . . . but I can't think of anything else to say about bees right now. I'm too busy contemplating my weary checkbook.

BeeAttitude for Day #30: *Blessed are those who drive slowly in residential neighborhoods, for they shall keep us bees safe.*

One thing I'm grateful for right now: *The sunlight filtering through the many healthy trees I have left.*

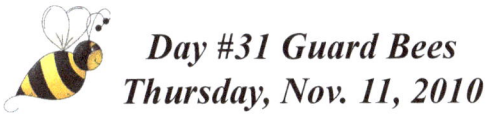

Day #31 Guard Bees
Thursday, Nov. 11, 2010

I thoroughly enjoy the meetings of the Gwinnett Beekeepers Club. Tuesday evening I learned that a hive's first line of defense is the **Guard Bees.** Sounds terrifying, doesn't it? Read on and you'll find out that it's NOT so scary.

When guard bees get alarmed—say you're approaching their hive too fast—do they sting you? Nope! Remember, if they sting you, they die. So instead, they go through this little routine of head bumping. That's right. They fly right at you and run into you—usually on your forehead.

That ought to be enough to warn you off. It sure would make me decide to wait until another time to check the hive. Luckily, I'm not going into this as a business, so if I can't harvest honey one day, I can wait until another day when the bees are calmer and it's no big deal. If I were using the bees as an income-producing work force, I might have to go ahead and open the hive even though I'd been head-bumped a number of times.

After the head bumping, if the person isn't smart, the guard bees get more serious. Hope I never run into that situation . . .

BeeAttitude for Day #31: *Blessed are those who learn our language, for they shall be sting-free (pretty much).*

One thing I'm grateful for right now: *Geri Taran, who is a bee-buddy of mine.*

Day #32 The Birds and the Bees
Friday, Nov. 12, 2010

No, I'm not writing about THAT. I'm writing about birds. And bees.

You see, they go together. A yard that is bee-friendly, with lots of nectar-producing plants, will probably be bird-friendly as well.

Some time ago, I started a running list of bee-friendly plants that I keep adding to as I think (or read) of new varieties. Viburnums and asters and zinnias and sunflowers. Bee balm (of course) and cleome and sages and daisies. Wax myrtle (male and female to get the fruits) and cardinal vine and Bachelor's Buttons. Beautyberry and blackberries and raspberries. And elderberries.

I already have a huge tulip poplar and a bunch of Rose of Sharons (Roses of Sharon?) in my front yard and an entire deciduous forest in my back yard. [**Added note in 2019**: The bees never once investigated the Rose of Sharon trees. They were here when I moved in. They self-seed prolifically and are of absolutely no value. I'd recommend you don't plant them.]

I'd love to get to the point where I don't need to feed the birds with purchased birdseed, but my yard simply isn't big enough for all those plants (not to mention the seventy others I have on my list). Birds need so much in the way of varied habitat. Bees are the same way. I'd like not to have to feed them sugar-water, but when I get that three-pound package of bees next spring, they're not going to have any honey stores to feed themselves or the babies that the queen will soon start laying.

That means I'll need to feed them.

So, I'll keep on going to Wild Birds Unlimited for my birdseed, and I'll crank up the sugar water when the time is right.

BeeAttitude for Day #32: *Blessed are those who plant yummy flowers, for they shall be surrounded by beauty and by happy bees.*

One thing I'm grateful for right now: *Miss Polly, the cat who is curled on my lap as I type. And Daisy, the cat who is perched on my shoulder. I know, I know -- that's **two** things for which I'm grateful. But there's no such thing as too much gratitude.*

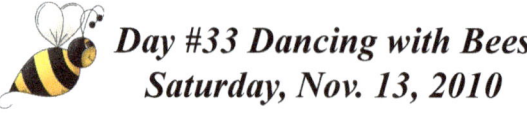 *Day #33 Dancing with Bees*
Saturday, Nov. 13, 2010

Well, I don't exactly dance with them. Not yet. But I'm looking forward to the time when I'll know that those forager bees are in the hive dancing their little hearts out.

It takes a high degree of cooperation amongst the members of a hive to collect, store, prepare, and protect the pollen, nectar, and eventually, the honey. If the older forager bees simply wandered around looking for nectar, there's a good chance the colony would starve, since good food sources that are relatively far from the hive might be visited by only a single bee,

like this one. The bees have it all figured out, though, which is one reason they've managed to survive so long. They dance. Now we all know dancing is good for you, but for the bees it's absolutely critical. When a bee finds a nectar source, she collects some, brings it home, and uses dance movements, either circles or figure-eights, to tell the other foragers not only that there *is* nectar, but also how far away it is, and in what direction.

The round dance tells the other bees that the nectar source is within 100 meters (that's 300 feet or so) from the hive, but the round dance can't tell the other bees which direction the nectar is in. For that information, they need the figure eight, often called the "waggle tail" dance for an obvious reason. The bee waggles her tail. The way she's lined up in relation to the sun gives the direction. And the speed of her dance tells how far away the source is.

So the foraging buddies head out exactly to where they've been directed, and find that patch of Michaelmas daisies, like the bright pink one above.

On cloudy days, the bees can still see the sun because they can sense ultraviolet light.

When another bee brings in info about a different source, she tell them which way to go, and more bees pour out of the hive to go get this new bunch of nectar.

Amazing, eh?

BeeAttitude for Day #33: *Blessed are those who dance in joy or in sorrow, for they shall find their direction in life.*

Something for which I'm grateful: *The fact that I can dance - as if no one were watching*

Day #34 Pollen Pockets
Sunday, Nov. 14, 2010

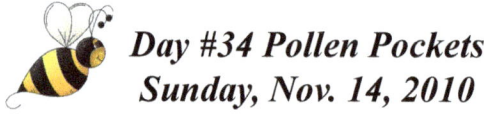

Way back on Day #14 I talked about corbiculae, the pollen pockets that bees have on the sides of their back legs. I've finally found some good pictures. I went to the Library of Congress website http://www.loc.gov/ and searched *public domain pictures*. Then I picked one of the choices they gave me (*animals*) and searched for *bees*.

That's why my posts recently have had so many photos in them. They don't come through with as much resolution as the originals, but you'll get the idea.

Here are a few that show the pollen clearly. See the sprinkles of golden pollen all over this bee's body?

And this photo shows the corbicula on her right back leg packed with pollen, like a little saddlebag:

BeeAttitude for Day #34: *Blessed are those who pay attention to details, for they shall have much more fun in life.*

One thing I'm grateful for: *The chance, occasionally, to experience different climates in this vast land of ours, and to know that bees are (almost) everywhere.*

 ### Day #35 More than eight thousand acres
Monday, Nov. 15, 2010

I keep getting more and more impressed with bees.

If foraging worker bees fly out **two miles** from their hive, the circle indicated by that radius encompasses 8,042.5 acres. That's a lot of pollinating.

Of course, if they can find ample nectar sources **within 100 yards** of the hive, *The Beekeeper's Handbook* says they have six and a half acres to cover. I'm making lists of the kinds of plants I can plant in my yard. We're at the end of the planting season here in Georgia, though, so my little bees are going to have to spread out a bit when they get started in the spring. I hope I can spread good bee-safety-energy around a few thousand acres.

Do bees have guardian angels?

BeeAttitude for Day #35: *Blessed are they who plant good food for us near our hives, for they shall have longer-lived bees.*

One thing I'm grateful for right now: *Oatmeal for breakfast*

Day #36 The Power of the Written Word to Eliminate Toilet Paper
Tuesday, Nov. 16, 2010

If you're a member of the Atlanta Writers Club you've already read something like today's blog, because I'm taking one of the "From the Tip of My Pen" columns I wrote for their monthly newsletter and adapting it a bit. Here it goes:

Over the past month, my life has taken quite a turn, and it's all - well mostly - because of two particular books: *No Impact Man* by Colin Beavan and *Animal, Vegetable, Miracle* by Barbara Kingsolver.

Colin decided he would try to live one year without making *any* environmental impact. Some of the life changes he made, such as no paper napkins or paper towels, are ones that I'd already adopted years ago, but I still have a long way to go.

He chose, for instance, to use no electricity. He, his wife, their daughter, and one dog lived in a ninth floor apartment in New York. No elevators (electricity!) meant an awful lot of stairs. No electricity meant no light bulbs. Locally produced candles solved that problem.

And no car. So they walked, biked, or rode scooters made from all used equipment. Did I mention that they vowed to buy nothing new (other than food from local sources)? And, they came out with a way to live without toilet paper. Don't ask me how they did it. Colin refused to give specifics in his books - he said it was too personal a topic.

So, I sat down and tried to figure out how they could have accomplished that. Why cut down trees to make a one-use product that will be flushed into the sewer, to be dealt with in a water treatment plant (which we pay for with our tax dollars)? I eventually developed a real good system. No, I'm not going to tell you how I did it. You'll have to come up with your own solution.

Then, the Kingsolver book changed the way I think about food. She and her family vowed to live an entire year on food that they had either produced themselves or that came from within their county. I've been telling myself for years that I should go to farmer's markets more often. For that matter, I know I should learn to cook, a skill that has eluded me since childhood. Listening to her (it was a CD version, read by the author), I saw the light. So, I've gone to farmer's markets and have signed up with a local food co-op so I can order SOLE food (sustainable, organic, local, ethical) and pick it up at Rancho Alegre in Dacula once a week. I made pickled beets a few weeks ago, and you would have thought I'd invented something divine. Don't laugh. A year ago I would have scoffed at the idea of pickling anything.

I won't belabor all the other changes I've made, but suffice it to say that the total effect has me feeling like a brand new person. All because of two books. All because of two writers. Pretty impressive, eh?

I can't claim to write words as powerful as Beavan and Kingsolver, although I do spend a great deal of effort revising until my novels say precisely what I want to convey. And I always try to include good information about bipolar disorder, suicide prevention, ethical treatment of animals, and even blood donations, for heaven's sake! Perhaps my work doesn't have quite the same impact as Beavan or Kingsolver's work, but I'm doing what I can.

And now that I'm getting into beekeeping, I have a feeling my next Biscuit McKee mystery will have little winged critters in it. Whatcha wanna bet?

p.s. When I first wrote this post (way ahead of time because I knew I'd be busy this particular day and wouldn't have the time to write it), I forgot to check the PUBLISH LATER box to schedule it for November 16th. Instead, I hit the PUBLISH NOW button, and sent it out to my devoted followers. So, you may have read this information once as an Atlanta Writers Club member, once as one of my followers, and once again today. If so, I applaud you. I promise not to goof again, unless I forget.

Fran Stewart

BeeAttitude for Day #36: *Blessed are those who live elegantly and simply, for they shall bee like us.*

One thing I'm grateful for right now: *The writers who have helped to shape the way I think.*

Day #37 Here's another bee joke
Wednesday, Nov. 17, 2010

I had so much fun with the last bee joke (see Day #24) that I want to do it again. Here goes:

Why did the bee cross the road?

Send me your answers, and I'll post the winner in a few days.

BeeAttitude for Day #37: *Blessed are those who love to play with words, for they shall be eternally entertained.*

One thing I'm grateful for right now: *The sunset last night and the sunrise this morning. Yes, yes - I listed* **two** *things, but it's my gratitude, so I can get away with it.*

Fran Stewart

Day #38 Tea and honey and good friends
Thursday, Nov. 18, 2010

I have a friend who likes tea as much as I do. She moved away from Atlanta quite some time ago, and I'm glad to say she's happy in her new place, but I miss her. Particularly when I sit down to have a cup of tea.

Before Kathi left, she and I visited Teavana, and bought an Imperial Blooming Tea Set. I think that's what it was called. Close enough. Anyway, it had two very tall silver-lidded jars, and two canisters of "blooming" tea balls. Those are made up of flowers surrounded by white tea-leaves, all of it hand-tied into a tidy little globular bunch. Kathi took one jar and one canister, and I took the others.

How does it work? I thought you'd never ask. You take a jar, pop one of the bloom balls into it, add hot water (if the water's boiling, it will make the white tea bitter, so be careful!) and watch as the ball swells, opens, and unfurls the flower buds within. *It's amazing, and lots more beautiful than those monster crystal things that grew in the bathtub when I was a kid.* Plus, you can drink the result. Of course, add honey first, preferably from local bees.

BeeAttitude for Day #38: *Blessed are those who sweeten their lives with friendship, for they shall find support when they need it.*

Some women I'm grateful for right now, women whose friendship I can count on: *Shar and Diana and Darlene and Millie and Debby and Cindy and Veronica and Geri and Nanette and Lyn . . . My gosh, I'm blessed indeed.*

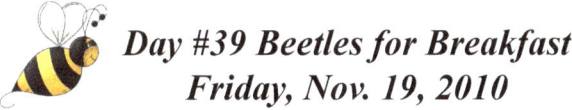

Day #39 Beetles for Breakfast
Friday, Nov. 19, 2010

Here are some things I'm thinking about:

bee types:
Italian Cordovan honeybees are gentle, and they make great honey.
Russian honeybees frequently have an attitude, but they make great honey, too.
Still, why would I deliberately choose grumpy bees?

beetles:
Bees in a hive that sits slightly elevated above a concrete slab have a better chance of defending themselves from SHBs (small hive beetles), since the housekeeping bees can grab the beetle larvae as they hatch and throw them out where they will proceed to roast on the sunny concrete (rather than burrowing down into the soil and multiplying).

breakfast:
I apologize if you're eating breakfast while reading this blog entry. You see, I write murder mysteries, and I have a cast-iron stomach when it comes to discussing poison, knives, bullet wounds, and other such gore over a meal. I have to watch myself in a restaurant lest the people at the next table call the cops after hearing me brainstorming about ways to kill off a character. So even something as awful as SHBs (and they *are* awful, considering what they can do to a hive of bees), is fair game as I sit here writing this post that will be published at 12:01 a.m. tomorrow. Whoops! Did I forget to mention that, as I type away, I'm eating Greek yogurt (from Cabot Farms) with cinnamon on it? And wondering . . .

Hmm . . . **Beetles could add some protein . . .**

p.s. Did you read Day #18? It's all about **cinnamon and honey**.

BeeAttitude for Day #39: *Blessed are they who eat a good and varied diet, for they shall be healthy.*

One thing I'm grateful for right now: *My adventuresome spirit and my openness to new ideas.*

 ### *Day #40 Whew! I'm home*
Saturday, Nov. 20, 2010

I keep hearing all this flap about not letting people on the internet know when you're not going to be home. Well, I took that seriously, so for the past week, I've been blogging from my sister's place in Colorado. We had a fun time together. We talked, talked, talked, laughed, laughed, laughed, and ate, ate, ate.

(Beth Stallings Photo)

Bees in a hive are all sisters (except for the drones, who get thrown out of the hive once winter comes). If I had a brother, I wouldn't do that to him. I'd want to be as good a friend to my brother as my son and daughter are to each other. But, back to my sister. Diana is an artist who has created a series of fabric art pieces (quilts/wall hangings/and such) that SHOW what depression feels like. The series she created is called "The Ragged Edge," and those twelve pieces hung at the Walter Reed Institute the summer of 1991 as a part of their DART (Depression Awareness/Research/Treatment) Program. She's currently looking for a museum or a corporation to display them in a permanent collection. Her talent continually astonishes me. She was diagnosed when she was in her forties, and has had twenty or so good years since then.

If you know anyone who is depressed (or who you think might be), please check out my sister's website http://www.depressionvisible.com/ and get her book *Depression Visible: the Ragged Edge*. I don't know whether bees ever get depressed. I would imagine they don't, but then again, how is one to know?

At any rate, Diana is a joy to be with now. While I was in Colorado, I took her to a meeting of the **Pikes Peak Branch** of the **NLAPW (National League of American Pen Women)**. What a dynamic group of people! I belong to the **Atlanta Branch** -- an equally powerful bunch of professional women in the arts. It's a delight to be able to talk with creative, artistic women, all of whom understand what we're going through as we strive to create our art, whether it's through words, music, paint, or clay. Rather the way all the sister bees in a hive cooperate with each other and appreciate each other's skills. I was buzzing with energy after the luncheon on Thursday.

After the long flight home, though, I feel sort of like a foraging bee must feel when she's flapped her little wings hard enough to carry her several miles from her hive and back home again. Do bees ever hang their tongues out and pant? For that matter, do bees ever sweat? Who knows?

My flight landed in Atlanta at 10:00 pm, and my friend Millie met me at the airport and drove me home. Bless her! I greeted my cats, wrote my gratitude list, wrote this blog, and then pretty much collapsed. What is it about sitting on an airplane that's so enervating? The lack of oxygen? The enforced inactivity? The proximity of so many overwrought people worrying about their schedules and fiddling with their electronic gadgets?

BeesKnees #1: A Beekeeping Memoir

Why can't we people be more like bees and simply do our jobs without the constant worrying? Worry wears our wings out.

BeeAttitude for Day #40: *Blessed are those who **look** while they fly, for they shall see the world from a higher perspective.*

One thing I'm grateful for right now: *My sister, Diana Alishouse*

Reminder: Check out her website to take a look at her art pieces that SHOW what depression feels like. While you're there, think about buying her book, Depression Visible, *for a friend who is depressed or who lives with someone who is bipolar. I never really understood what my sister was up against until I read her book.*

 ## Day #41 Singing is Like Buzzing
Sunday, Nov. 21, 2010

As I write this, it's 6:30 Saturday evening. I just got home from an all-day rehearsal for the Gwinnett Choral Guild, and boy, did I have fun. [**2019 Note:** The GCG disbanded several years ago—a great loss to the community and to me.] I simply love singing with that group. The conductor, Phillip Shoultz, is dynamic and exacting, and kind at the same time. He can pull music out of us that we didn't know we had in us. I enjoy being held to a high standard of excellence (is that phrase redundant?)

We're getting ready for some upcoming concerts, rather like bees preparing for the winter. They gather honey -- we gather song. They dance -- we sing.

We're going to do our annual Messiah Sing-along on the Sunday after Thanksgiving at Lawrenceville (GA) Presbyterian Church. Come on along and sing a hallelujah or two.

"But, I live in Texas," you say. Or in Louisiana or Michigan or Australia. Well, just as there are bees practically everywhere (except Antarctica), so there are singers. Check out your local high school. I bet their music department is putting on a concert of some sort.

After you hear the singers, tell me all about it.

Just 129 more days until I get my bees! Do you think you can stand waiting that long?

BeeAttitude for Day #41: *Blessed are the singers, for they shall have rich lives indeed.*

Two people I'm grateful for right now: *Veronica and Millie, who cared for my cats while I was in Colorado.*

 Day #42 How about four (or even five) winners?
Monday, Nov. 22, 2010

So, the question (on day #37) was: Why did the bee cross the road?

And I couldn't decide who should win. What do you think? Here are the answers - in the order I received them:

Just bee-cause.

Because "A Taste of Honey" was showing at the drive-in theater across the road.

Because the chicken wanted to.

Bee-thoven was playing in the concert hall across the road and over the hill.

Bees don't need a reason. They just have to bee.

Duh! The hive was over there, dude.

Now, I ought to warn you that three of these answers came from one family, which is one reason I wouldn't dare pick a winner!

BeeAttitude for Day #42: *Blessed are those who are kind to chickens. Those birds need all the help they can get.*

One thing I'm grateful for right now: *My furnace, installed six years ago by Cool-Ray, and still running just fine. (Brrr! It's cold outside!)*

Fran Stewart

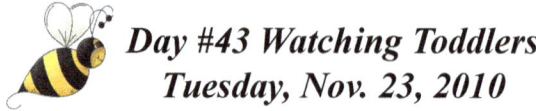

Day #43 Watching Toddlers
Tuesday, Nov. 23, 2010

Well, a dear young friend of mine asked me to babysit her and her two toddlers Monday. She's extremely restricted for the next few months, until her baby is born. Don't you love it when the doctors tell the mother of two small boys not to lift A N Y T H I N G ? Hmmm . . . Don't think I could have managed that years ago when my kids were small.

Although, come to think of it, when my children were 2 and 5, my appendix ruptured. I thought it was a torn muscle and walked around for ten days caring for my children until I was finally way too sick to function. By the time I went for a check-up, I had peritonitis. Probably should have killed me—but it didn't. The emergency room people were appalled that I had driven my kids to a sitter and then myself to the hospital. This blogger is one tough cookie!

The kids I watched this time around were a delight. Two loving, happy, bright little boys. I had a great time and laughed enough to make my sides sore.

I wonder if bees love each other? Is hive discipline the same thing (sort of) as two parents who lovingly teach their children? I don't know. What do you think?

BeeAttitude for Day #43: *Blessed are those who raise their children well, for they shall be doubly blessed when they are old farts (like our beekeeper).*

One thing Fran is grateful for right now: *Her sense of humor.*

 ## Day #44 Reaching Across the World
Wednesday, Nov. 24, 2010

On Tuesday, I mailed some of my books to two people I'd met through the Internet. One is working on her Doctor of Divinity degree; we correspond through emails and Skype. I may be editing her work, but I'm also learning a lot from her.

Another is a science writer who works for NASA. I subscribe to NASA Science News, and I kept noticing her name listed as the author of articles I truly enjoyed reading. Finally one day, after reading her explanation of "Curiosity" (a space exploration vehicle trudging over the dusty Mars landscape), I clicked on her name. Ah-ha! A link to her email. So I wrote her a quick note about how much I had enjoyed that particular article. She manages to get wry humor into most of her articles. In this one, she'd said that exploring Mars was much like finding your grandmother's dusty journal in an attic. Of course you'd read it! And you'd find out that "Granny was a pistol."

Here's what I said to her in my first email after I introduced myself briefly:

I am so impressed when I read a scientific article that is as lucid as yours was. Your image of exploring grandmother's dusty diary was truly brilliant. The "bird-dog" simile was equally effective. Thank you for your meticulous detail and your fine writing. You're going on my gratitude list tonight because of the joy I felt reading about "Curiosity."

Best wishes,
--Fran

p.s. I have read my grandmother's diaries -- and she WAS a pistol!

She replied and, over the past year we've kept up quite a conversation. She finally got around to reading my first mystery, and then asked me to send her another one. The same thing happened with the doctoral candidate in Australia, who is working her way through every one of my books.

Well then, where do bees come into all this? Think about the folks who emigrated from the Old world to the New World in the 17th and 18th centuries. I'd be willing to bet some of them were beekeepers. The sailing ships then were rather like the Internet now. They carried letters (emails). They allowed forays into new realms (like Internet searches). The beekeepers, finding bees in the Americas, would have recognized them and their value, much the same way I recognized value in the NASA article and the dissertation.

Queen bees, on their maiden flight, go to where the drones gather (a new territory indeed for the young queens) and mate with a large number of drones from differing bees hives (colonies). They bring the resulting genetic variety back to their hive in the same way that ideas from the New World mingled with ideas from the Old.

So - pull out your granny's old diary. You never know what you'll find. Maybe she kept bees.

BeeAttitude for Day #44: *Blessed are those who explore new worlds, for they shall find nectar in abundance.*

One thing Fran is grateful for right now: *My connections with Mesheril and Dauna*

 ### Day #45 The Post Office
Thursday, Nov. 25, 2010

Two days ago I went to the post office to mail a package to a friend in Australia and some books to the Bartram Trail Regional Library in Washington GA. They'd bought some of my books, and I told them I'd donate some others. I love libraries. Anyway, while I waited in line, one of my favorite postal workers, Debbie, told a man at the counter that the way to measure a box was along the longest side and then all around the shortest way. How on earth would anyone ever remember that? But then she added, **"Head to toe and around the waist."** Don't ya' love it?

The bad news was that the postage for four books to Australia was over $40. On the other hand, what's the cost of flying a really long way? I guess $40 is well worth it, since hand-delivery would be impractical.

Bees never have to worry about that sort of stuff. They gather their pollen and nectar within a five-mile radius of their home hive. Of course, large commercial beekeepers transport hives all around the country on huge flatbed trucks to follow the large commercial crops, rather like my flying to Australia to deliver a present of books. Wouldn't it be nicer if we encouraged bee tending all over the country? Think of it. Every house with a hive or two. Every orchard or garden with dozens of them. Let the bees do their thing. Don't worry about medicating them. Don't use pesticides on the crops. Don't try to force honey production.

I know – that's a Mother Earth News kind of mentality – and there are plenty of folks who simply aren't interested in keeping bees or eating pesticide-free food. But, just for a moment – imagine! Wonderful, isn't it?

BeeAttitude for Day #45: *Blessed are they who, like our field bees, deliver gifts, for they shall rest assured that their hive is safe.*

One thing Fran is grateful for right now: *The nice people at the Lawrenceville Post Office on Buford Drive.*

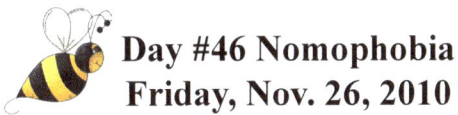
Day #46 Nomophobia
Friday, Nov. 26, 2010

I found a new word! *Nomophobia*. It certainly wasn't in my *Webster's Seventh New Collegiate Dictionary* (published about forty years ago). Usually that old blue book serves my logomaniacal needs just fine. But English is an evolving language, and we need new words.

Hence dictionary dot com and *nomophobia*. That's a fear that probably creeps up rather often in theaters and at large family gatherings—if the family matriarch insists on the turning off of cell phones. *Nomophobia*, you see, is "the fear of being out of cell phone contact"—certainly not a fear that ever affected me growing up and doesn't worry me now. You see, I enjoy solitude. I am quite capable of leaving my phone behind when I go The Shakespeare Tavern or a Thanksgiving dinner. That way I can thoroughly enjoy the conversation.

Bees don't have to worry about nomophobia or any other kind of fear. They do their jobs efficiently and quietly (except for the buzzing). That's why I spent part of Thanksgiving Day simply sitting on my deck imagining what the bees and the hives would look and sound like when they're operating next spring. I had a cup of my favorite Tazo Chai tea in hand, and a good book manuscript to read (the one I'm writing!) What could be better?

BeeAttitude for Day #46: *Blessed are those who are complete unto themselves, without electronic gadgets, for they shall be able truly to enjoy the moment.*

One thing Fran is grateful for right now: *Thanksgiving leftovers*

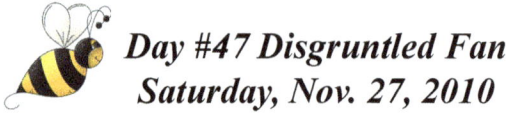
Day #47 Disgruntled Fan
Saturday, Nov. 27, 2010

Friday I received an email that said: "Why didn't you talk about Thanksgiving on Thanksgiving Day?"

Good question. For one thing, even Google put a roast turkey and a pumpkin pie on the home page that day. Don't get me wrong; I appreciate the fact that we set aside a day for football—uh, I mean for giving thanks—but I tend to give thanks every day of my life. That's why I include a gratitude statement in my blog each day. That's why Biscuit McKee, the librarian in my mystery series, writes a gratitude list at the end of each day. That's why Marmalade, the library cat, adds her gratitude list (*leftover chicken, the bird feeder, gentle pats, being brushed, this soft chair*).

So, for the Thanksgiving Day blog, I talked about the Post Office. If that struck you as being disrespectful, I apologize.

One of the things I've been most thankful for recently has been my getting to know bees better. If you've read my posts with any regularity, you'll know that they have me learning, growing, philosophizing, laughing, and waxing thoughtful about my place in the Universe. Bees have been around a very long time—140 million years or so—much longer than dinosaurs, turtles, and/or hominids. If I can help make their life a bit easier in my little corner of Georgia, then I have every reason to be thankful.

BeeAttitude for Day #47: *Blessed are those who inquire, for they shall find answers.*

One thing Fran is grateful for right now: *You - for reaching out to ask your question.*

 ## Day #48 The Family History of Bees?
Sunday, Nov. 28, 2010

Bees don't need genealogy. When 80,000 bees in the hive are all sisters and have the same mother and won't be having children themselves, it seems a little silly to chart them.

I suppose serious bee breeders like to know where their queens come from. I'll be buying a particularly gentle breed of bees next Spring, and I suppose I'm glad the bee farm people know what they're doing, but the bees themselves couldn't care less.

They know when a queen is failing—not laying enough eggs—and they get rid of her and create a new queen. Then the new one flies off and mates with whatever drones she finds in the drone-gathering place. Those drones have congregated from miles around—no telling what their genetics are.

So, after a while, my gentle bees will probably evolve into their own little family with traits that I might not have counted on when I got the original batch. That's life, folks. And it's a logical consequence of "natural beekeeping," letting the bees do what they do naturally. Come to think of it, the new queen *might* mate with drones that are even **gentler**. Wouldn't that be great?

I've read in several bee books that if an undesirable trait *(such as bloodthirstiness)* crops up, it's my job as a bee-keeper to isolate the queen and - - - gulp! - - - squoosh her. I don't know if I'd be able to do that. Hopefully I'll never have to find out.

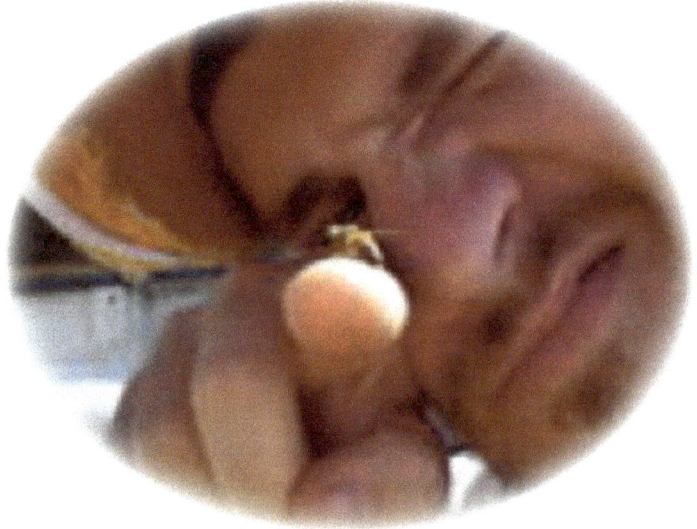

If I do—you'll read about it here, and you'll just have to imagine the teardrops spotting the page.

For now, though, all is well on Frannie's back deck. Of course, there aren't any bees there yet.

BeeAttitude for Day #48: *Blessed are those who let well enough alone, for they have a much simpler life.*

One thing Fran is grateful for right now: *My granddaughter who called me on Thanksgiving Day. Remembering our conversation lightens my heart.*

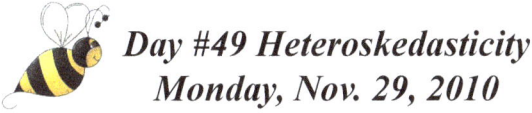

Day #49 Heteroskedasticity
Monday, Nov. 29, 2010

I wonder what a doctoral dissertation for a bee would involve?

As part of my work as a free-lance editor, I work with people from all over the country, editing their dissertations. A couple of days ago, one of the dissertations mentioned "heteroskedasticity-consistent tests." Try to say *that* six times really fast. I will say, in defense of the doctoral candidate, he hadn't used the word himself. It was simply cited in his reference list as part of an article title.

Not only did I have to look it up so I'd know whether or not it was spelled right (you can apparently substitute a c for the k and still be correct), I was curious as to what it meant. Once I knew that, I began to wonder what words a bee would use to sound really important in her thesis. Here are a few I came up with:

Nectargrination: flying all around the place to find flowers that have enough nectar to be interesting.
Queenification: the process of eliminating a weak queen and producing a new one.
Beebreadify: To bring beebread (a rich mixture of pollen and various liquids) down from the storage cells and feed it to the baby bees.
Cleansidepoopifidumpification: Taking the queen's waste products away from her and depositing them outside the hive.
Scrubbadubbadadeck: What Frannie will have to do next summer after a lot of cleansidepoopifidumpification has been going on.
The next time I edit a master's thesis or doctoral dissertation for a bee, I'll know whether or not these words are spelled right.

BeeAttitude for Day #49: *Blessed are those who spend their whole lives learning, for they shall either be a fountain of wisdom or a fountain of trivia.*

One thing Fran is grateful for right now: *Sesquipedalian words that make me laugh*

Day #50: I'm getting worried
Tuesday, Nov. 30, 2010

I keep thinking about getting that package of several pounds of bees in late March or early April.

I've watched the YouTube videos and the DVD from my bee-supplier. They all show a confident looking beekeeper turning the box upside down and—POW!! hitting it against the hive to dump the bees out forcibly.

I can't do it. I've tried to see myself cracking that screen-sided crate against the hive, and I get cold shivers just thinking about it. The beekeepers say the bees don't mind. HA! How would they know? Did they ever ask the bees? If I were a bee, would I want to be slammed into my new home? NO, NO, and once again, NO!

Instead, I think I'll just move some of the frames out of the way, open the package of bees, and set it inside. They'll figure out where their queen is fast enough.

If you're an experienced beekeeper reading this and you think I'm nuts—well, that's what the comment section is for. Go ahead and tell me I'm wrong. I'll listen . . . but when April gets here, I might not heed your instructions.

BeeAttitude for Day #50: *Blessed are the gentle.*

One thing Fran is grateful for right now: *The run-off election here in Gwinnett County GA*

 ## Day #51 Drone Facts and Philosophy
Wednesday, December 1, 2010

- Adult drones, unlike worker bees, have no stingers, so drones can't sting. Worker bees, with their barbed stingers, die when they sting someone or something. But drones are so fat and sassy they don't need to sting anyone. Their danger zone comes about when an unmated queen flies up to a drone gathering. She'll mate with 20 or 30 drones—and the poor guys literally explode at the end of the mating process.

It's never failed yet: whenever a man hears that fact, his comment (following a chuckle) is always, "Well, at least they die happy."

- In a **natural beehive**, drone cells (the ones that are larger than worker cells) are grouped around the bottom and sides of the hive frame. When a queen is ready to lay an egg in a large cell like that, she chooses a non-fertile egg. Yes, she can tell the difference. That non-fertile egg grows into a drone. The eggs for the worker bees are laid in a spiral pattern starting near the center of the frame. Some beekeepers think the bees waste too much energy creating all those drone cells and drone larvae, and some go so far as to cut off the drone cells. But, guess what? The workers will just build more drone cells. Why?

Well, I've read that if a predator breaks into a hive, it will generally start eating the comb at the edges. Voila! The drones are there to serve as sacrificial hive-savers so the worker larvae are more likely to survive.

- Drones in the late fall are a sorry lot. You see, each drone eats an inordinate amount of honey, and a hive couldn't survive the winter with the non-productive fellas eating up their food stores, So, as the weather turns colder, the workers force the drones out of the hive and dump the drone brood (the unhatched baby drones) out the front door. And I thought my book *A Slaying Song Tonight* was gruesome! It's nothing compared to this mass murder.

- The good news is that as winter comes to a close, the queen begins laying eggs for both workers and drones that will mature shortly before the new workers are needed for the upcoming spring nectar and pollen. The drones that emerge get to eat a lot and go flying around, where they gather with other drones and buzz-buzz-buzz about guy things, until along flies a brand new queen. And then . . . well, they die happy.

BeeAttitude for Day #51: *Blessed are the drones, for they shall contribute to the survival of the hive.*

One thing Fran is grateful for right now: *The rain that is filling the pond a mile or so from my house.*

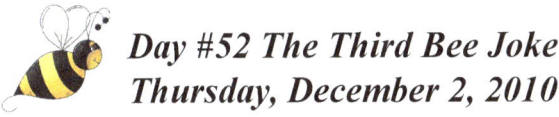 ***Day #52 The Third Bee Joke***
Thursday, December 2, 2010

Okay. We tried ***How can you tell if a bee is hyper*** (day #21) and ***Why did the bee cross the road*** (day #37).

Now it's time for: A bee's favorite musician is ___ (*fill in the blank*)

Email me your answer(s).

Be thankful I didn't ask: *Who's a bee's favorite astronaut?* [groan]

BeeAttitude for Day #52: *Blessed are the folks who make good movies, for their work is appreciated.*

One thing Fran is grateful for right now: *The movie "Ladies in Lavender"*
 [Can you tell what I was doing Tuesday evening?]

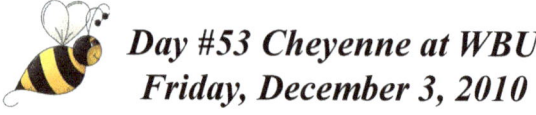

Day #53 Cheyenne at WBU
Friday, December 3, 2010

There is absolutely nothing like a greeting from a friendly dog. Every time I walk into Wild Birds Unlimited on Lawrenceville-Suwanee Road, you'd think I was a queen. I stock up on birdseed there on a real regular basis, so the store dog is used to me.

After a few I'm-so-happy-you're-here wags, Cheyenne, a big yellow-lab sweetheart of a dog, flops down to get her tummy rubbed, as if I were the only person alive who does it just right.

Cheyenne, from Wild Birds Unlimited

My bees aren't going to do that next year when I get them installed in the hives on the deck. I imagine they'll notice me when I approach the hive. They may even get used to having me around, but you need a dog for the kind of attention Cheyenne gives. On the other hand, Cheyenne doesn't create honey that I can steal.

Still, she did give me a WBU 2011 Calendar and my very own little package of Poop yesterday.

No-no-no, it's not what you think. This Poop is a snack product from Columbia Empire Farms in Oregon, and the label says (I kid you not): **Yellow Lab Poop / Chocolate Nut Toffee / net wt. 4 oz. (113g)**

Ya gotta love a dog that would think of that.

BeeAttitude for Day #53: *Blessed are dogs, for their love shall heal people.*

One thing Fran is grateful for right now: *Local businesses run by people I admire, respect, and enjoy*

p.s. I discovered a really cool Bee Person: check out http://www.beeweaver.com/ and take a look at the little video called "Saving the Honey Bees - Hour of Decision." [2019 Note: When I checked this link I could no longer find that video – but the website is still full of a lot of great information about bees.]

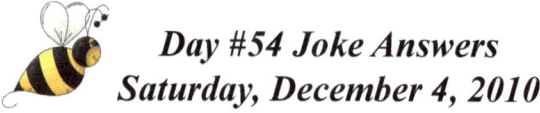

Day #54 Joke Answers
Saturday, December 4, 2010

I got more responses about the astronaut joke (Who is a bee's favorite astronaut?) than I did the fill-in-the-blank one. Everyone who emailed me about the astronaut said—of course—"BUZZ Aldrin."

As to the other question, *A bee's favorite musician is _____*, the answers were evenly matched between:

Sting and Bee-thoven

I guess you all win!

BeeAttitude for Day #54: *Blessed are those who fly into space, for they shall see beauty.*

One thing Fran is grateful for right now: *Those of us who stay on the ground and STILL manage to see beauty.*

 ## Day #55 Baby Goats and Baby Bees
Sunday, December 5, 2010

Did I ever tell you about the baby goat I got to feed once?

It happened when I was doing some research for *INDIGO AS AN IRIS,* my fifth book in the Biscuit McKee mystery series. I located a goat farm in Watkinsville GA and asked if I could come watch the goats and ask lots of questions. Mandy Lattimer said yes, so I went, learned lots, finished my book, and then went back the next spring to see the goats who had been pregnant when I was there the first time.

Okay, I admit it—the real reason was to see **baby** goats that had just been born. It takes a few days for baby goats to get used to nursing, and in the meantime the moms fill up with LOTS of milk, so Mandy milks the mamas, puts their milk in bottles, and feeds their babies until the little guys can get the hang of how to do it on their own.

I was there at just the right time, and I got to help! The baby I fed—one day old and cute as the proverbial button—was highly enthusiastic about eating, but wasn't quite sure what to do with that rubbery thing I kept poking in his mouth. He kind of had the idea that it was the food source, but getting a grip on it was more than his little goat mouth could manage.

The result? Almost as much milk on me as in him. Mandy's much better at it than I am. You see—it wasn't entirely the little fella's fault. I didn't know how to hold the bottle at the right angle. It had been a long time since I'd had to feed a baby (and a four-legged baby at that!)

The guard dog had his eye on me the whole time.

Now, bees don't have that problem. For one thing, no mammary glands. The babies eat their way out of the cells, shake themselves, dry off a bit, and start to work. None of this gamboling about like goats (yes, the baby goats did these cute little hip-hop dances around and over everything). Baby bees are all business.

I just re-read that last sentence. I wonder if I'm wrong. Surely the newness of life is a joyful experience for a little bee coming into a hive full of supportive sisters and one great big mama.

Next spring, I'm going to try to watch the babies and see if they bounce around a bit before they start cleaning the cells.

BeeAttitude for Day #55: *Blessed are they who hunger and thirst for knowledge, for they shall be pleasantly surprised.*

One thing Fran is grateful for right now: *The incredible opportunities that have come to me as a writer.*

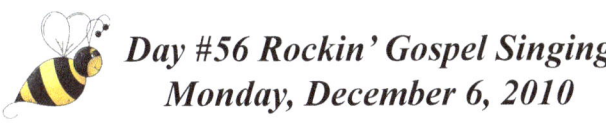

Day #56 Rockin' Gospel Singing
Monday, December 6, 2010

Well, Saturday and Sunday were great fun. The Gwinnett Choral Guild gave two concerts. The music was challenging, and I was astonished at how much sound came out of my old lungs. We just got started singing and sang our hearts out.

In case you're interested, we started with three different versions of the *Magnificat*. High-falootin' stuff. Organ music—which I can't stand, so don't ever give me an organ CD, but I must admit the volume was impressive.

Then we sang some more traditional Christmas songs—*White Christmas, Sleigh Ride*, things like that—interspersed with performances by the Georgia Young Men's Ensemble, a phenomenal group of young guys from 6th grade through high school (and even a couple of college guys who enjoy singing with the group so much, they keep on attending rehearsals).

We ended up with yet another Magnificat—this one *The Gospel Magnificat* by Robert Ray. Soul music at its best. We had the place rocking both concerts. I ended up energized and exhausted both. Love singing with that group!

Have I mentioned that I plan to sing to my bees once I get them here? I think that makes sense. I wonder if they'd prefer classical or jazz? I'm pretty good at elevator music, too, but if they want rock or rap, they'll have to hear that in somebody else's back yard.

BeeAttitude for Day #56: *Blessed are those who make music, for we shall enjoy their buzzing.*

One thing Fran is grateful for right now: *Singing—and having more music pulled out of me than I knew was in there.*

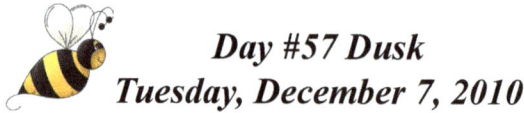
Day #57 Dusk
Tuesday, December 7, 2010

All the animals I know slow down at dusk.

Why don't people do the same? It's quarter to eleven on Monday night as I write this—to be published tomorrow morning (which means about an hour and a half from now).

I just got home from a wonderful rehearsal.

I thoroughly enjoyed myself.

AND - I'm pooped!

When the sun goes down, why don't we?

Are bees smarter than we are?

BeeAttitude for Day #57: *Blessed are they who pace themselves, for they shall last longer.*

One thing Fran is grateful for right now: *The energy to do what I love to do.*

Day #58 Poor bees - they can't read
Wednesday, December 8, 2010

One of the greatest joys of my life has always been *reading*. From the time I was just a little tyke, books have shaped my world. No matter what was going on, I could find companionship, or solace, or good advice in a book. What a shame that bees don't read. What a shame they don't write, either.

Think about the books they could publish:

Memoirs:
The African Queen
The Drone Mutiny

Non-fiction:
Hive: the Inside Story
Cell: the Inside Story
Beebread: from pollen to nutrition

Historical:
As It Was in the Beginning: Our Life Before Dinosaurs
The Agony and the Extra Bee

Documentary:
The Culprit Behind Colony Collapse Disorder
Skunk Attack: How One Hive Survived!

Mystery:
B is for Bees
One for the Honey
Brown as a Wing Vein

BeeAttitude for Day #58: *Blessed are the readers, for they shall never bee lonely.*

One thing Fran is grateful for right now*: All my mysteries are available as e-books now.*

Fran Stewart

Day #59 Art by Grandkids and Bees
Thursday, December 9, 2010

As I write this, I'm looking at two pictures drawn by my grandchildren. The bright colors and the sheer imagination -- all of this delights me.

I think bees draw pictures, too. The queen bee lays her eggs in a beautiful spiral pattern, like the seeds in a sunflower. This means that as the eggs go through their various stages, those cells change in the same spiral pattern, each of them progressing from an open cell with a single skinny white egg at the bottom of it to one with a growing pupa, and on to the point where the workers pack the cell with honey and pollen for the larva to eat as it continues its growth. Eventually the workers "cap the brood," covering it over with a yellowish-brownish wax cap.

Like an artist picking different oils (or, in the case of my grandchildren, crayons and pens), the bees choose a different color wax to cap the honey cells. That's how a beekeeper knows for sure which frames hold the white-capped honey.

Of course, as the baby bees mature, they emerge in that same spiral pattern, the first-laid at the center and the newer ones progressively outward. Finally the queen goes back to the center and starts over again with yet another first white egg in a newly-cleaned cell.

The fact that they've been doing it this way for 140 million years doesn't make it less artistic. It's beautiful. Do they do it because they "have" to? Well, yes, I suppose so. But maybe each queen considers her options and says, "Spirals! That'll look gorgeous!" And we have a continuous wax canvas in front of us.

BeeAttitude for Day #59: *Blessed are those who choose to see beauty around them, for they shall be uplifted.*

One thing Fran is grateful for right now: *Hot oatmeal on a cold morning.*

Day #60 More book titles from the bees
Friday, December 10, 2010

Well, if there's one fan of BeesKneesBeekeeping who is keeping me in stitches, it's Petie from Houston. She and her whole family take this blog to heart. I've gotten more comments from Petie than from anybody else. On day #58, when I was talking about Bee's Book Titles, she came up with:

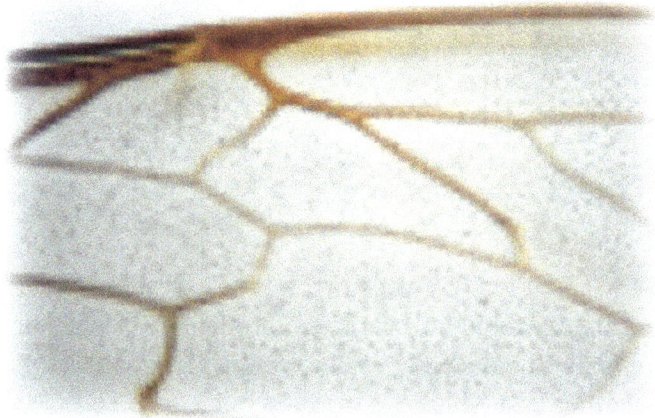

Gone with the Wing

Inherit the Hive,

and

To Hive or Hive Not

I dare you to top these!

And for some reason, nobody's groaned out loud yet about *The Agony and the ExtraBee*. I thought it was pretty funny . . .

BeeAttitude for Day #60: *Blessed are those who like to play with words. We're not sure why, but they seem to laugh a lot, and they send off healthy vibrations that we bees can sense.*

One thing Fran is grateful for right now: *People who write very clear instructions. (It's an art that isn't always followed.)*

[Photos are from the public domain, except for the "Rubber Duck Yellow Hive" from H & L Bee Farm]

Day #61 Stability and Slumgum
Saturday, December 11, 2010

How long does beeswax last?

Well, *The Beekeeper's Handbook* tells me that it is stable for thousands of years. I'll keep that in mind.

I also need to know this: when I'm melting beeswax in my solar melter (the one I guess I need to build), old comb won't melt as well, and will form a dark, gummy residue called **slumgum**. (No, I am not kidding.) I can put it in my compost pile. Well, that's encouraging.

Does that mean that if I came across an old stash of beeswax, say from the time of the pharaohs, it would all be slumgum? Does "old" mean "used many times and therefore contaminated with dirt, oils, pollen grains, and such?" Or does "old" in this case simply mean "well-aged"? I don't know. The book doesn't say.

But, the next time I come across some really old, old beeswax, I'll melt it and see if I have the making of candles, cosmetics, floor polish, car polish, furniture polish, adhesives, crayons, chewing gum, ski wax, or even some kinds of ink.

Or will it just be a big lump of slumgum?

BeeAttitude for Day #61: *Blessed are the archaeologists, for they shall live in wonder of the ancient world.*

One thing Fran is grateful for right now: *The rich dark soil I get from my compost pile.*
And one other thing - the folks at http://www.beeweaver.com/, commercial beekeepers who avoid using chemicals on their bees. I like that attitude! Their queens are resistant to varroa mites.

 ### Day #62 The Joy of a Good Heater
Sunday, December 12, 2010

My car has one.
　　My house has several.
My bees . . . ? Well, they have each other.

Now, you know I don't actually *have* the bees yet. But my imagination is rife, and I can practically see the little ones flying in and out of the hives right outside my bay window.

But not on a day like today. Brrr ! ! ! ! !

The bees cluster together and shiver, thereby generating heat. One bee alone can't possibly keep itself warm by shivering, but when they all group together, the heat-to-bee ratio goes way up, and they can keep a hive at a comfortable temp, as long as nosy beekeepers don't open the hive on the first sunny day to "check on" the bees.

BeeAttitude for Day #62: *Blessed are the beekeepers who leave us alone most of the time, for we shall reward them with great sweetness.*

One thing Fran is grateful for right now: *The space heater next to me.*

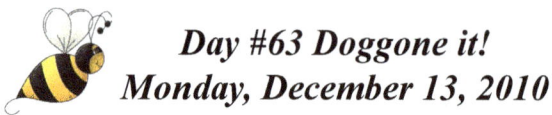

Day #63 Doggone it!
Monday, December 13, 2010

Well, for somebody who's normally as healthy as a bee, I sure did manage to come down with a whooper of a cold. As long as we don't stress bees out, they do pretty well, so what happened to me? I don't think I'm stressed out:

I'm happy.
I have good friends and wonderful family.
My cats are healthy (i.e. not barfing up hairballs or anything else).
All my editing jobs are caught up, and I'm getting four new clients starting next week.
My books are (FINALLY!) out as e-books.
My checkbook is balanced.
I have plenty of food to last through the upcoming cold spell.

I could go on with the list, but you get the idea. I don't have a reason to be stressed. Still, I have a cold. Yuck!

I'm someone who believes that we *create* our circumstances, and that what we see in the world is a reflection of who and what we are. So, I must be wanting to honk at somebody, if my nose is any indication.

Trouble is, I don't think I'm mad at anybody.

What would the bees tell me to do?

BeeAttitude for Day #63: *Blessed are those who take care of themselves gently, for they shall get better faster.*

One thing Fran is grateful for right now: *The hot water, lemon juice, and **(thank-you bees!)** honey I'm drinking to ease my sore throat.*

Day #64 I'd rather be singing
Tuesday, December 14, 2010

Well, Monday night was a dress rehearsal for the Gwinnett Choral Guild, singing at Brenau University in Gainesville with the Gainesville Symphony Orchestra. Tonight (Tuesday) will be the performance. I'm missing both of them. Phooey!

How do opera singers ever manage? Surely they must get an occasional cold. Or maybe not.

Yes, I apologize. I'm still whining about feeling sick.

So, what is there about bees that will cheer me up?

-They are a sunny yellow, just like my bathroom walls. I like yellow.
-It's only about 14 more weeks until I get to pick up my nuc and my package of bees.
-Worker bees do a wag-tail dance to identify where the nectar is. I could dance around my living room just for the heck of it, and that would keep me from grumping about my sore nose.
-On days when I can't sing myself, I'll be able to step outside and listen to my hives!

Okay. I feel better now. Will somebody tell my nose to keep up with me?

BeeAttitude for Day #64: *Blessed are the singers, for they shall be filled with joy.*

One thing Fran is grateful for right now: *Hot water.*

 ## Day #65 A little chat
Wednesday, December 15, 2010

I was chatting with a friend of mine a while back. She told me how much she enjoyed looking at flowers.

No! Not that friend. It was a different one.

© *Yelloideas Photography*
And not that one either, although I'm sure he enjoys flowers as much as anyone.

Yes! Finally, here's the one I was talking with.

She was telling me how special flowers are to her, and I said, "Then you have a lot in common with the bees I'll be getting next spring."

"Bees?" she queried. "They're those noisy, fuzzy little critters, aren't they?"

"Well, I don't know about noisy, but they do have fuzz on their bodies."

"Believe me, sweetie, you haven't heard noise until you've really listened to a honeybee." But then she paused and considered. "You're a human, aren't you?" she asked. "Humans are even noisier than bees. Maybe you could take a few lessons from them."

"Thank you," I whispered, and tiptoed away.

BeeAttitude for Day #65: *Blessed are those who are quiet, for they shall hear more.*

One thing Fran is grateful for right now: *My son, who takes such interesting photos and lets me use them on my blog.*

Fran Stewart

 ### Day #66 The New York Times talks bees
Thursday, December 16, 2010

What's the *New York Times* doing in my blog? I'm still not over my cold, so I'll let the *New York Times* speak for me in this article about the value of bees in New York City (and elsewhere).

Here's the article a friend of mine from Arizona shared with me. (Thanks, Ellen!) [2019 Note: The article disappeared.]

And to answer the questions you sent in about what the critter in the first picture in yesterday's post was:

It's a **Porcupine Puffer Fish**, photographed somewhere in or around the Philippines by my son (data-base-manager / circus-performer / fire-spinner / lamp creator / master scuba-diver / all-around good soul).

Enjoy the *Times* while I have a cup of hot tea (with **honey**, of course).

BeeAttitude for Day #66: *Blessed are good reporters, for they shall enlighten their world.*

Something Fran is grateful for right now: *The map that shows me it's one L and two Ps.*

 ## Day #67 The truth about assassins
Friday, December 17, 2010

I learned the truth about Assassin Bees when Bill Dunn spoke at the most recent meeting of the Beekeepers Club of Gwinnett.

You never heard of Assassins? Sure you have—just not under that name.

For a while the press called them **Killer Bees**, which sounded much more exciting than their original name. Then, for some unbeknownst reason, the name shifted to **Africanized Bees**.

Now, who's to say that some of the feistiness of those critters isn't a good thing for bees in general? I don't know.

But they really are **assassins**. And the way they work is fascinating. Want a gruesome tale of treachery that rivals that of the Trojan Horse?

You DO recall the details of *that* story, don't you? It's the reason people began saying, "Beware of Greeks bearing gifts." The Greeks appeared to be losing in their long siege of the city of Troy, so they built an enormous wooden horse, left it in front of the gates, retreated to their ships under cover of darkness, and sailed out of the harbor.

"Look!" the Trojans cried the next morning. "A gift from our defeated enemy!" *They shoulda known better.*

They rolled the wheeled horse into their city and celebrated like crazy, getting dead drunk in the process. Along toward dawn, Greek soldiers who'd been hidden in the belly of the wooden horse jumped out and opened the city gates. The inpouring army slaughtered . . . well, you get the idea.

Assassin Bees are even smarter than that, though. They form a cluster in a tree somewhere in the general vicinity of a regular beehive. The cluster is to protect their queen, who is in the center. Then they send out scouts, who forage for nectar and pollen. The scouts fly up to the unsuspecting hive, land on the front door, and display their gifts.

"Gee, thanks!" the guard bees say. "You wanna bring us presents, we'll accept." Gradually the number of assassin bees within the hive increases, until there are enough to launch an attack on the resident queen.

After they've killed her, the swarm breaks up, flies to the hive, and installs their own queen. Pretty as you please. And the original worker bees don't put up a fight because, once their queen is dead, they're toast, unless they get a new queen quickly. Voila. Assassin Queen to the rescue.

You know what they say: "Beware of Bees bearing gifts."

BeeAttitude for Day #67: *Blessed are the gift-givers, for they shall prosper.*

One thing Fran is grateful for right now: *My chiropractor, who straightened out my wrist when I fell on the ice.*

Day #68 The solstice lunar eclipse
Saturday, December 18, 2010

Bees and the night sky? Bees and the moon? Bees and astronomy? Bees and the Solstice? Bees and photography?

Lunar eclipse Nov 2003 Photo Credit: Jim Fakatselis

I can't think of a way to connect this blog-post to the general topic of bees, but I'm going to post it anyway because I think the topic is pretty interesting.

If you read this blog regularly, you know I subscribe to **NASA Science News.** I'd like to share with you this great article about the **total lunar eclipse** that will be visible on the night of the Solstice (the night between December 20th and 21st).

The article explains why the moon glows **an eerie red** during a lunar eclipse and exactly when to see it. The photo above comes from the NASA article. http://science.nasa.gov/science-news/science-at-nasa/2010/17dec_solsticeeclipse/

If you live anywhere in North America, you'll be able to see the eclipse—if you're willing to take the time. If the skies over Georgia will cooperate by staying cloud-free, I plan to take a look.

I know it's possible to see a lunar eclipse despite the light pollution of a city area, because the following two photos were taken by my son from a balcony in light-filled downtown Atlanta during an eclipse in November 2008.

Yelloideas Photography

I've seen only a few eclipses, but each one has been memorable indeed.

If you see the one next week, let me know what you think.

BeeAttitude for Day #68: *Blessed are those who look up, for they shall live in wonder. We bees wish we could see the moon; it sounds marvelous.*

One thing Fran is grateful for right now: *Those precious few places in this country where light pollution is not a factor.*

 ***Day #69 Bees, rain, and geese***
Sunday, Dec. 19, 2010

Saturday morning it rained and rained and rained.

If I were a bee, I'd have a problem with that. Bees with wet wings can't fly. That's why some beekeepers spray their bees with sugar syrup to calm them down. I'm not sure it calms them; it simply immobilizes them.

So, what am I going to do next spring when I get my bees if it rains for days on end, the way it did in Atlanta last year? Feed them, for sure, and hope they have the good sense to come in out of the rain and stay dry.

The trouble is, I like cloudy, rainy days. It's my vitiligo—I have no melanin in my skin, so I can't tan, and I sunburn easily. That means that what I like is different from what my bees will like.

I don't even have them yet, and I'm worrying about them like a mother goose clucking at her goslings.

Quack!

BeeAttitude for Day #69: *Blessed are those who plant lots of flowers and vegetables, for their yards shall be well pollinated.*

One thing Fran is grateful for right now: *Sunny days in the winter and cloudy days in the summer.*

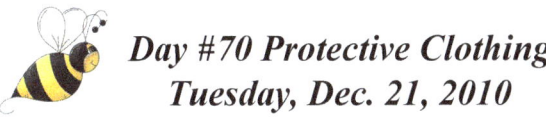

Day #70 Protective Clothing
Tuesday, Dec. 21, 2010

"There is no stigma attached to wearing protective equipment; it will save you and your visitors a lot of worry if you are properly prepared to look through colonies without the fear of being stung."

So says *The Beekeeper's Handbook*, which I've quoted numerous times in this blog. I was caught by that phrase "there is no stigma." And I disagree with it. Having talked to a lot of beekeepers over the past few months, I've noticed that the ones who say, "Of course, *I* never use veils" generally have an underlying pride in those words, as if they belong to an exclusive club, the Anti-Veil Society.

"You can use a veil if you're afraid," they say. "I just scrape out the stinger and keep working." Or "Don't be ashamed if you have to use a veil," when what their tone implies is "Shame on you."

Well, until I'm really, really used to my bees, I *will* use a veil, without any feeling of inferiority. The risk of receiving a sting on my eyelid (or getting an inquisitive bee stuck in my ear) is a bit more than I can stand.

I'll be buying veils in the next few weeks. I did buy three used veils—a real mistake, as they turned out to be in need of such major repairs, they're not worth the effort. I wonder if I could ask for my money back?

BeeAttitude for Day #70: *Blessed are those who ask for what they need, for they shall receive.*

One thing Fran is grateful for right now: *Warm curtains over cold windows.*

 Day #71 The Perfect House
Wednesday, Dec. 22, 2010

Six or so years ago, I was looking for a house. I wanted it to be smaller than the one I was living in at the time, with a certain arrangement of rooms, a two-car garage, lots of trees, a front porch that was such and such a size, and so on. My long-suffering realtor took me around to see numerous prospects, none of which fit the bill.

Finally, one day in absolute desperation, I climbed into his car and said, "I've upped the ante. I want a house with everything I've had on my list PLUS I want a skylight, a wood-burning stove, and a bay window." While he gaped at me, I added, "And a creek in the back yard."

We looked at five houses that day. The first had a skylight; the second had a bay window; the third had a creek; the fourth was a disaster. I bought the fifth house, which had everything I asked for. Little did I know, when I gave him that list, that someday I'd be sitting here in my bay window looking out at the big back deck where the bees are going to be installed.

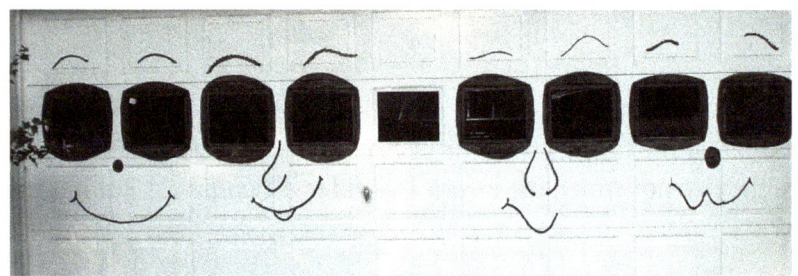

Fran's Garage Doors

Oh! And did I see the lunar eclipse Monday night? Yes indeedy! The moon was so bright when I got up to go outside at 1 a.m. that I pulled my rocking chair under the skylight, leaned back, and watched in total comfort as the moon passed into the shadow of the earth, until the reddish glow was quite apparent. At which point, the clouds swept in and I couldn't see anything else. I was warm, and happy. What more can one ask?

BeeAttitude for Day #71: *Blessed are they who are open to new experiences, for they shall be pleasantly surprised.*

One thing Fran is grateful for right now: *The people who've bought my e-books.*

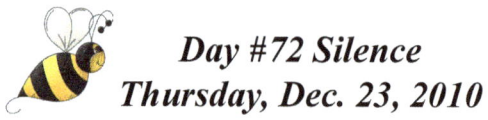

Day #72 Silence
Thursday, Dec. 23, 2010

There are so many kinds of silence:

A quiet day at home
A night of despair at a hospital
Watching the eclipse in wonder
Sitting near my beloved grandchildren as they draw
Holding a dying cat
Knitting
Seeing the first crocus in late winter
Crying with a friend
Holding my breath while a deer walks by
Marveling at the 43-year-long marriage of two dear friends - (How did they do it?)
Sitting with a purring cat warming my lap
Reading and, of course,
Writing

Each of these silences has its own quality. Some are happy; some are not. In the spring, I'll be able to add:

Listening to my bees

I'm looking forward to it.

What are *your* kinds of silence?

BeeAttitude for Day #72: *Blessed are those who refrain from talking, even for a little while, for they shall eventually* hear.

What Fran is grateful for right now: *Miss Polly, curled in my lap, and the memory of Panther, who died in my arms two years ago today.*

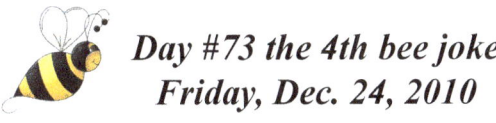
Day #73 the 4th bee joke
Friday, Dec. 24, 2010

Okay, answer this one: What did the *(fill in your choice of occupation)* say to the bee who was tired?

Send me your answers. I wonder who's going to win?

BeeAttitude for Day #73: *Blessed are those who enjoy the work they do, for they shall be fulfilled.*

One thing Fran is grateful for right now: *The pumpkin bread that's making the house smell so good as it bakes.*

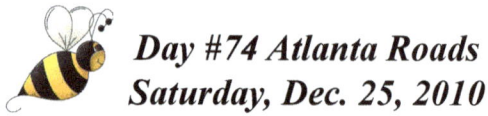 ***Day #74 Atlanta Roads***
Saturday, Dec. 25, 2010

December 25th is just about the only day that I can drive down I-85 at any time of the day without seeing more than 2 dozen cars at a time, if that many. I know because I've driven it a couple of times over the past 18 years that I've lived in Atlanta.

Today, though, this particular beekeeper will ignore the nearly bare interstate and drive the three miles to my daughter's house to see her and all the grandchildren. I'll take the pan of pumpkin bread I baked yesterday for dessert, and the Dilly Crackers for snacking. (Let me know if you want the recipe.)

Whatever your plans for today, I wish you well.

BeeAttitude for Day #75: *Blessed are you, truly.*

What Fran is grateful for right now: *Family and friends*

 *Day #75 Making Christmas Simpler*
Sunday, Dec. 26, 2010

Decorating for the holidays, any holidays, is not my strong point.

I'll tell you a story if you promise not to laugh at me. On second thought, I'm deleting that request. Laugh all you want to, and then send me your favorite Christmas story. Laughing is good.

In December of 1968, eleven months after I'd gotten married, the days crept forward with no tree, no lights, no bulbs, no tinsel. On Christmas Eve, my husband and I looked at each other and said, "Why hasn't Christmas happened?" We'd both been so used to having the trappings of Christmas appear around us, that it never dawned on either of us that now we were responsible for it.

A rude awakening, as we found out that a holiday requires a fair amount of planning. We rushed out to the tree-sellers, and came home with what was left—a bedraggled little pine that conveniently was missing most of its back side, which meant we had room to walk past it into our tiny dining room. Woolworth's provided (for an exorbitant $1.29) a huge box of red ornaments and a measly string of white lights. We forgot about a tree stand, and we didn't have a bucket, so we nailed a couple of boards to the bottom of the trunk, and had ourselves a merry little Christmas.

Needless to say, all the needles fell off before December 27th and wedged themselves in the carpet (I hadn't known about the real reason for tree skirts). The next year, I planned a little better, and all the holidays gradually became elaborate decorative affairs. It was a heck of a lot of work. Did I enjoy it? I don't really know. I did it, pulled along by the stream of expectations.

Eighteen years ago, though, I adopted a cat. She was fine with the first Christmas tree she'd ever seen. So was Kreo, the next cat the following year.

Then I moved to Georgia, and Waldo wandered into my garage one day, bleeding and starving. By the next Christmas, Waldo taught the other cats what Christmas trees were REALLY for. The next year, with two more rescued cats in the house, I braced the tree with string attached to cup hooks screwed into the woodwork around the windows. The following year (during which there'd been another couple of cat-rescues) rope replaced the string and sturdy metal eyelets replaced the cup hooks. I must admit that seven cats perched in one tree looked rather festive. Until several branches broke and the tree fell over. Wish I'd had a camera.

The next year I gave up on Christmas trees. December is so much more relaxing now.

BeeAttitude for Day #75: *Blessed are they who enjoy all the seasons without too much fuss.*

One thing Fran is grateful for right now: *Phone service so I can call my sister on any given holiday—and any other time as well.*

 ## Day #76 Lion Fish and Carolina Wrens
Monday, Dec. 27, 2010

I looked out my bay window yesterday when I heard the distinctive trill of a Carolina Wren. She hopped from a bush of indeterminate lineage (which simply means I haven't yet figured out what kind it is) up to the deck railing, and from there to the rim of the bird bath. She (he?) looked up at me in a meaningful way, so I scooted outside and refilled the bird feeders, then came back inside to watch the antics of the chickadees and wrens and woodpeckers and all that assortment who know that a sucker lives in this house.

That's the sort of thing I look at on a regular basis, and next spring I'll be able to add bees to my routine.

My son, on the other hand, looks at things like this:

Lion Fish by Yelloideas Photography

and this:

Table Coral by Yelloideas Photography

from places like this:

Inside the Boiler of a Wreck by Yelloideas Photography

Can you see why I like to be where I am, enjoying his peripatetic ramblings on my computer and my phone? And watching my birds (and eventually, the bees) from a place of warmth and space?

BeeAttitude for Day #76: *Blessed are the adventurers - and blessed are those who stay home, for we shall both enjoy our nature encounters.*

One thing Fran is grateful for right now: *Hot tea*

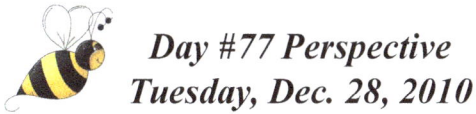
Day #77 Perspective
Tuesday, Dec. 28, 2010

Every year, along about this time, I sit down and read through my journal for the year, jotting down the things I've accomplished. Each year has its high points. You know what my next sentence will be—the one about the low points, so I'll skip writing that.

The point I'm trying to make is that reviewing a year is a good way to put life into perspective. Just for the fun of it, though, I dug out some of my old journals and (GASP!) saw for sure why I'm happier to be **here and now** rather than **there and then**.

Some of my years have plodded along, while others have raced; but most of them had one or two (or more) shining moments. For 2010, I'd have to say my shining moment was the time I spent at the **Southeastern Vipassana Meditation Center**. A week and a half in silence. Not just *no talking*, but no eye contact, no gestures, no sign language, no physical contact, no singing, no phone, no writing, and no reading.

I was okay with the ban on speaking, and had no problem leaving my cell phone locked in their office, but the ban on reading and writing just about did me in. I came within a hairsbreadth of bailing out a couple of times. Thank goodness I stayed. There is something almost magical about shutting up for ten days and simply *being*. We worked hard, getting up at 4:00 each morning, meditating for two hours, breakfast, meditation, walking, meditation, lunch, meditation . . . You get the idea.

The fact that I stayed, went on my accomplishment list, for sure. And out of that silence came my beekeeping. Yes, that's what I said. During the first day's meditative walk, I spotted a honeybee, watched it forage through a patch of wildflowers, and said a silent goodbye as it flew away. Three steps farther on, another bee, and another, and another.

Each day I looked forward to walking the nature trail and observing the bees. I began to see that there was something concrete I could do for my patch of this earth. Something that would nourish me in more ways than one. Honey, yes. But something so much deeper as well. A way to help heal the earth.

I found (and on the last day when we *could* talk, the other women admitted that they too had discovered) that without ever looking at each other, we began to recognize each other's footsteps. We felt such gratitude to the unknown woman who broke needle-laden twigs from a fallen pine tree to lay across one muddy stretch of the walking trail, interspersed artistically with dead palm fronds like many-fingered hands. If we'd been able to talk, I dare say we'd have complained a great deal about the mud. As it was, we saw her gift, and each of us began to find ways in which we could serve the greater community.

The lessons in meditation were at times grueling, as I fought my own stubbornness and came to grips with some issues that had plagued me for years. But the end result was well worth the effort.

If I listed nothing else except the Vipassana course and the decision to keep bees, my accomplishments list for 2010 would feel complete.

BeeAttitude for Day #77: *Blessed are those who see bees in silence and wonder, for they shall find new worlds opening to them.*

One thing Fran is grateful for right now: *Beekeeping supply catalogs to browse through*

 ## Day #78 Introductions
Wednesday, Dec. 29, 2010

Two Honey Bees

I love introductions. That's where most authors say what they really want to say, the way I did on Day #1 of this blog. In most books, the intro sets the tone of what is to come.

As I browsed yet again through *The Beekeeper's Handbook* yesterday, I thought to re-read the intro. Diana Sammataro, who co-authored the book, wrote:

Although considered to be a "gentle art," beekeeping in reality can be physically demanding and strenuous. The typical picture of a veiled beekeeper standing beside the hive ... does not show the aching back, sweating brow, smoke-filled eyes, or painful stings.

Worker Bees and Capped Brood

And I went ahead and decided to try beekeeping anyway, although I still have not figured out how to get my smoker to stay lit. Four more months to practice!

Come May, June, and July, I hope I'm still singing the praises of bees. And I hope I'll eventually have some honey to make up for the ache, the sweat, the smoke, and the ouchies.

BeeAttitude for Day #78: *Blessed are they who persevere, for we shall produce honey enough and they shall be rewarded.*

One thing Fran is grateful for right now: *People who write truly helpful books.*

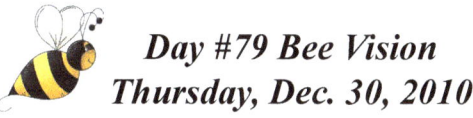 Day #79 Bee Vision
Thursday, Dec. 30, 2010

Don't count on red flowers to attract bees. Bees can't see them.

I know. That surprised me, too, when I read it in *The Beekeeper's Handbook.* Bees, apparently, can see orange, yellow, blue-green, blue, violet, and ultraviolet (the last of which we mere humans cannot see). Plants that need bees for pollination will most likely have flowers in this color range. If they don't, they're out of luck, for the honeybees will pass them by.

My first objection, when I read the list of acceptable colors was, "Wait a minute! I've seen all sorts of photos of bees on white daisies." Smart me? Nope! Take a look at these pictures:

White petals, yes, but look at those great big **ORANGE** centers.

I still plan to plant some red *Lonicera sempervirens,* though. For the hummingbirds!

BeeAttitude for Day #79: *Blessed are the artists, for they shall dance with color.*

One thing Fran is grateful for right now: *The enthusiasm of my grandkids as we made cookies last Monday, and the rocks they decorated for me*

 ## Day #80 Happy New Year's Eve
Friday, Dec. 31, 2010

Do you ever wonder how animals manage to adapt to fireworks?

We used to have dogs who freaked out so much they tore apart the inside of the car one New Year's Eve when we were dumb enough to take them with us to the fireworks display.

Now my cats get wide-eyed when the various booms and crashes go off, although they tend to take their cue from my sense of calm and finally settle down to—what else?—a cat nap.

I saw a bird scared off her nest on my front porch one Fourth of July by neighborhood firecrackers—and her babies died in the cool night air, since most songbirds have no night vision to speak of and can't find their way back to the nest.

I generally read late into the evening, since it's hard to sleep with the explosions a mile and a half from my house. The next morning I wake up happy and greet the new year.

No matter how you choose to spend this evening, I hope you'll say a little prayer for the frightened animals.

BeeAttitude for Day #80: *Blessed are they who refrain from scaring us, for we shall live longer and make more honey for them.*

What Fran is grateful for right now: *The past year, the year to come, and this very moment.*

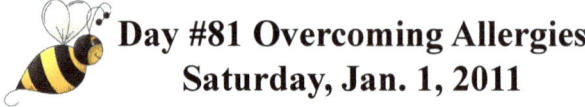 Day #81 Overcoming Allergies
Saturday, Jan. 1, 2011

I know, I know. On January first I'm supposed to say "Happy New Year, and may 2011 be filled with prosperity." There. I said it.

What I'd rather say is, "Joy surrounds you. May 2011 be the year you discover the truth of your inner joy." There. I said THAT.

Now let's talk about allergies. I was glancing back through my journal from a couple of years ago, looking for something else altogether, and I came across a note about a friend who underwent injections of bee venom to alleviate a serious allergy to bees. Took five years, but it eventually worked. My point is, I suppose, that no matter what confronts us, there IS a way to deal with it.

So, maybe I should have said, "May 2011 be the year we find an open doorway for every one of our possibilities. And may they all be good ones."

Happy 1-1-11(!)

BeeAttitude for Day #81: *Blessed are those who search for their own truth, for they shall find doors aplenty.*

One thing Fran is grateful for right now: *My brand new, safe, clean water heater, installed by Keep Smiling Plumbing.*

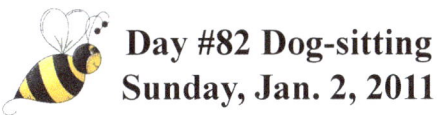 Day #82 Dog-sitting
Sunday, Jan. 2, 2011

Why have I not been talking a whole lot about bees recently? Well, for one thing, it's cold outside, and this time of year bees spend their time in a cluster keeping themselves warm. I'm spending an inordinate amount of time keeping warm myself, since I've been in a writing frenzy recently, and sitting at my desk doesn't get the blood circulating.

I've also been dog-sitting, driving 3 miles each way twice a day to feed and water Belle and Max. And, of course, go on poop patrol with them. I wish I could truly appreciate just how much information these dogs can amass through their noses. Sniffing EVERYTHING is a mission, a purpose, a calling. Or maybe it's just that everything smells so *much*.

I wonder how bees smell?

I remember sniffing my own forearm a lot when I was a kid, intrigued by the scent. I tried to talk my mother into sharing the joy once, but she turned up her nose and didn't comply. So I had to laugh last night when Belle sniffed one particularly odorous (for her) patch of grass and then looked up at me as if to say, "Okay, it's your turn now." I, like my mother, declined, even though I couldn't see any noticeable poop-lumps there. Now, sitting here, I wonder what new world might have opened to me if I'd knelt down and put my nose to the earth.

I think I'd rather just imagine it instead of doing it.

BeeAttitude for Day #82: *Blessed are they who are open to new experiences, for they shall be happily surprised. Go smell some dirt, Frannie!*

One thing Fran is grateful for right now: *The boundless enthusiasm of Belle and Max, and their joy when I walk in the door.*

 Day #83 Bee-you-tiful Bee Joke Answers
Monday, Jan. 3, 2011

Back on Day #73, I asked What did the *(fill in your choice of occupation)* say to the bee who was tired?

Here are some of the responses:

The runner said, "It's all in the knees" (bee's knees!) -- *from Bill*
The pilot said, "Bee-keeping your wings up!" -- *also from Bill*
Another pilot told the bee to "straighten up and fly right!" -- *from Sal*
The hairdresser said, "Honey, that beehive is totally you!" - *from Billy*
A different hairdresser said, "Where's your comb?" -- *from Petie*
The builder said, "Your propolis needs propping up." -- *from Connie*
The chiropractor said, "Let's line up your wing and your sting." -- *from Marsha*
The midwife said, "Pop out of it, Sweetie!" -- *from Jan*
The inspirational speaker said, "Focus on what's right about you, and you'll bee just fine." -- *from Ellie*
and the final one:
The proctologist said, "All you need is a cleansing flight." -- *from George* (Note from Fran: I'll explain this one in a later blogpost.)

Thanks to everyone who commented or emailed. I thoroughly enjoyed the answers!

And I'd like to acknowledge all of you who've tried to become followers or to make comments, but haven't been able to make it work. I have no idea what's wrong. I probably set the blog up wrong somehow, but don't know what to do about it. If anyone has a suggestion, please let me know.

BeeAttitude for Day #83: *Blessed are the beekeepers, for they shall bee happy.*

One thing Fran is grateful for right now: *The gorgeous sunset through the storm clouds last night*

Fran Stewart

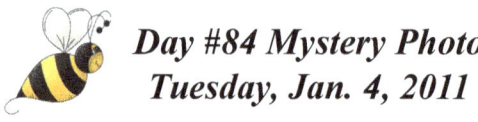

Day #84 Mystery Photo
Tuesday, Jan. 4, 2011

The reason I'm using this picture is that it has sort of the same colors as bees, and looks like it has some of the same texture, too.

Can you guess what it is? It took me a LONG TIME to figure it out . . . First one to identify it correctly wins a jar of **Bee's Knees Honey** (although you'll need to wait until I get my bees and they start producing enough for me to -- er -- borrow some!)

photo credit: Yelloideas Photography

BeeAttitude for Day #84: *Blessed are the whimsical, for they shall always see similarities to fuzzy bees*

What Fran is grateful for right now: *My children and grandchildren*

Day #85 Pea Soup and Sweet Peas
Wednesday, Jan. 5, 2011

Miss Polly, my alarm cat, is 14 years old. She's lived with me since kittenhood. And this week, for the very first time, I found out that she likes pea soup. You'd think in more than a dozen years I could have figured that out. But, come to think of it, I doubt I've cooked pea soup since I left Vermont 17 years ago.

Anyway, last Saturday I was sitting at the computer, writing. I'd placed my empty bowl of soup off to the side. Polly jumped onto the table, pounced on the bowl, and licked it clean.

Was it a brand new taste for her, or had she perhaps nosed through some garbage when she was a teeny kitten, and found the leavings of a pea-soup meal so that the smell of *my* pea soup activated a long-forgotten memory?

And then, the other day I was getting together a bunch of old gardening magazines (from 2006, but the information in there is still good) to donate to the American Kidney Services. They'd called me and specifically asked for magazines. Naturally, I browsed through a few of them before filling the (BIG) box, and I noticed pictures of a plant I haven't thought about in ages.

It's not that I don't know about these plants. It's just that they bypassed my radar somehow when I moved into this house six years ago. As soon as I saw the picture, though, I practically pounced on the idea of planting sweet peas. I whipped out my White Flower Farms catalog, and the one from Wayside Gardens, and found that to get sweet peas, I'll have to plant seeds. That's fine with me.

Sweet Petey Pie by Tami Landis

I couldn't find a public domain picture of a sweet pea flower. This is the closest I came.

Why a dog? Well, when I typed "sweet pea" or sweet pea flower" in the search box, they gave me a picture of sweet potatoes, one called "sweet tooth" (a photo of frosting-topped doughnuts), candy, and -- would you believe it? -- a mango. And this dog. But all of this is beside the point. Let's get back to memories of tastes.

I got to wondering whether bees who have never seen a sweet pea before are surprised when one of their foragers brings the nectar into the hive, and all her sister worker bees say, "Yes! Great new taste!"

Or does the memory of sweet pea nectar go back through millions of bee generations? Does the hive simply *know* that sweet peas are good because bees have been pollinating them for millions of years? When I have sweet peas flowering in my yard next spring, will the forager bees see them and say, "FINALLY!! It's about TIME somebody planted those things again!"

If only I spoke *BEEnglish*. Then I'd know the answer.

BeeAttitude for Day #85: *Blessed are those who remember the good things, for they shall encounter them again.*

One thing Fran is grateful for right now: *Garden catalogs and submarine sandwiches*

Day #86 Explaining the Joke from Day #83
Thursday, Jan. 6, 2011

In the #83 blog I promised to explain that final joke, which was:

What did the proctologist say to the tired bee?

Answer: "All you need is a cleansing flight."

I hope you have a strong stomach if you're eating breakfast right now.

Try to imagine what would happen to the floor of a beehive (whether it's in a hollow log or in a beekeeper's wooden box) if all the bees pooped indoors all the time? Not a pretty thought.

So, bees poop on the fly, and usually each little summertime contribution is so tiny we'd never notice it. But right after winter? That's a different matter. Think about it. Those poor little critters have been clustered inside the hive all winter long to keep themselves warm, and they haven't—er—eliminated anything.

So imagine the first warm day of spring, with bees pouring out of the hive. Now imagine the ground around the hive as those bees take what is euphemistically called their "cleansing flights."

BeeAttitude for Day #86: *Blessed are those who raise vegetables near our hives, for they shall benefit from our fertilization.*

One thing Fran is grateful for right now: *The new garden plans I'm putting together so I can take advantage of bee fertilizer! I hope they fly over the garden more than over my deck . . .*

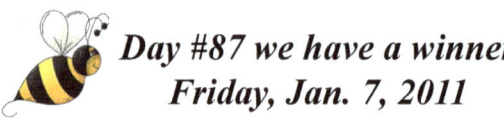
Day #87 we have a winner
Friday, Jan. 7, 2011

Go look at the mystery photo on day #84. We have a winner who identified it over breakfast that day.

For correctly identifying the **giraffe**, Cathy Akers-Jordan wins a jar of my Bees Knees Honey whenever I get around to:
- getting my bees,
- learning how to work with them,
- figuring out how to take the honey away from the bees, and
- managing to get it into jars without sticky-ing up my entire house.

Naturally, the bees are going to have to cooperate in this endeavor by doing their nectar thing.

BeeAttitude for Day #87: *Blessed are the teachers, for they help to create a better world.*

One thing Fran is grateful for right now: *Artichokes with hollandaise sauce*

Day #88 I Think I'm Going to Have a Problem
Saturday, Jan. 8, 2011

I was sitting here yesterday looking out the bay window, idly trying to decide how to resolve a scene in the new mystery I'm writing, when I noticed the leaves on the deck.

"Yeah," you say, "so what?"

Well, my house is surrounded by trees, so I get a lot of lovely shade in the summer, which keeps the house relatively cool in the Georgia heat. My highest electricity bill last summer was $47. There are pines to the north and south of my house, but on the west, there's nothing but tertiary deciduous forest in my back yard. And there's this season called Autumn.

I'd swear that every tree west of me dumps its leaves on my deck. They do it pretty much all year round—trees drop some leaves even in the summer, and there are several kinds of trees, like the beeches, that hold onto their leaves and wait to drop them in the spring (which is when my bees will be getting started).

That translates to a lot of leaves on my back deck. I'm pretty sure there must be a miniscule trade wind that swoops through the trees way back beside the creek and swirls them over here. "Oh look! A deck! What a great place to drop this load of leaves!"

Now, normally, the fallen leaves provide exercise for me throughout the spring and summer and fun for my grandkids in the autumn when they sweep leaves into big piles before we transfer them to the compost pile. Fine.

I took my hive outside, though, to see what it would look like on the deck. It's certainly going to mess up my sweeping pattern. And two or three of them will make it even harder. I'll have to place the hives far enough away from each other and from the deck railing that I'll be able to get my big broom in between them. I hope the sweeping won't bother the bees, because that big wide broom is hard to control. I'm always bumping it into things. I don't think the bees will like it if I bump the hive.

Good grief, Fran! Just use a narrower broom.

Oh. In that case, forget it. I guess I don't have a problem.

BeeAttitude for Day #88: *Blessed are those who plant trees, for they shall breathe better.*

One thing Fran is grateful for right now: *The tulip poplar that graces my front yard. (Tulip poplar trees produce flowers that honeybees love!)*

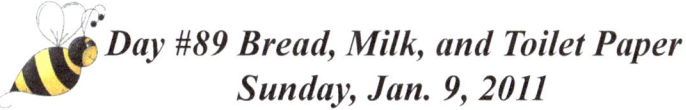

Day #89 Bread, Milk, and Toilet Paper
Sunday, Jan. 9, 2011

I've noticed in the seventeen years I've lived in Georgia, that whenever there's a snowstorm predicted, people flock en masse to grocery stores to buy three particular items. Not only do they buy it—they buy it in huge quantities.

Saturday afternoon I drove to Publix on my way home from seeing *Amahl and the Night Visitor*, and found the parking lot jammed. All the grocery carts were in use . . . ALL of them. I grabbed a basket and plowed through the hordes to buy my four little items. I wish I'd had a camera as I walked past the empty shelves on the bread aisle, and the likewise empty shelves where there used to be toilet paper. The milk cooler looked vacant.

I don't drink cow's milk, and I already had some goat's milk on hand. I make my own bread usually, and I gave up toilet paper months ago (see blog for day #36 in November).

Nice to know I didn't have to shove anybody out of the way in the Publix aisles!

BeeAttitude for Day #89: *Blessed are those who plan ahead, for they shall not be caught lacking.*

One thing Fran is grateful for right now: *Recorded Books*

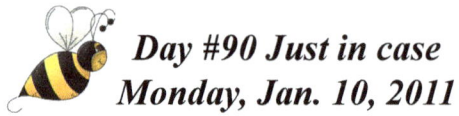

Day #90 Just in case
Monday, Jan. 10, 2011

How much time do we spend doing things "just in case . . ."?

It makes sense to stock food and water and candles just in case of a weather problem.

It makes sense to have a pencil handy just in case I'm somewhere without access to a computer.

It makes sense to get an extra hive body (the box the queen bee lays eggs in) ready just in case my bees multiply faster than I think they might.

It makes sense to save a percentage of income each month just in case I'll need it in the future.

And yesterday morning, it made a great deal of sense to me that just in case the power goes out in the stupendous snow and ice storm that was predicted to hit Georgia Sunday night, I should write these blogs ahead of time for the next few days. Eight years ago, a big branch from a pine tree fell and snapped my power line, and I was the only one in my neighborhood without power during a particularly nasty ice storm. Naturally I was LOW on the list of priorities for the power company. They were trying their best to get electricity to hospitals and nursing homes and neighborhoods where *everyone* had lost power.

I made it through by living in one room with the nine cats I had at the time. It's amazing how much heat a cat generates. We slept under a tent of blankets. I ate cold food. I lit a dozen or so big pillar candles in the adjoining bathroom—put them in the tub and propped up a screen door so the heat could get out of the room and the cats couldn't get near the candles.

Nine days later, my power was back on. I must admit that the eighth day I walked up the street and asked a neighbor if I could sleep in her spare room. She fed me hot food, too. She hadn't known I was having such a hard time.

As you may know, because I've mentioned it often enough in these blog posts, I have a grove of huge pine trees on the north side of my house. That's where the line comes in from the power pole, so I'm being sensible. I'm writing blog #90 and the next few as well while I'm sitting here warm and comfortable. Then I'll schedule them to post at 12:01AM on the appropriate days.

Just in case...

BeeAttitude for Day #90: *Blessed are the sensible, for they (like bees) shall prepare for winter.*

One thing Fran is grateful for right now: *Hot Cream of Wheat*

 Day #91 Bees in Eleven Weeks
Tuesday, Jan. 11, 2011

Happy 1-11-11 !-!!-!!

After writing yesterday's blog about *planning ahead -- just in case*, I looked at my calendar and did some counting. I'll be driving to south Georgia in just eleven weeks (or maybe twelve, depending on when H and L Bee Farm has them ready) to pick up my honey bees.

The trouble is—I don't know what the heck I'm going to do with them when they're here. Oh, I know lots of bee theory. I've read dozens of books and perused multiple Internet sites about beekeeping, written by highly knowledgeable beekeepers. Part of me feels prepared. And part of me is scared speechless.

You know what I'm having the most trouble with? Lighting the blinkin' smoker. Smokers can be fancy copper, or utilitarian steel. I'm showing you a picture of each. Mine's the steel one.

A beekeeper uses smoke to calm bees before opening the hive. A smoker is a special gadget that provides a place for the smoke-producing fuel, a spout to funnel that smoke out in a particular direction, a bellows to push air into the fuel chamber to increase the amount of said smoke. That's about it.

Those suckers get hotter than you-know-what, so one is advised to have some handy bricks or a concrete block nearby on which to set the smoker once the bees are settled down.

It needs to be nearby so the beekeeper can quickly add more smoke as necessary (in case the bees get a bit of an attitude).

Fine.

How the heck do you keep the thing lit?

I've watched videos about it. I've read descriptions of what to do. I even watched an experienced beekeeper light a smoker when I was first getting interested in keeping bees. So, I know how to do it, right?

Tell that to the incalcitrant smoker sitting on the bricks on my back deck. I can't get it to keep burning. I get one or two big poofs of smoke out of it, and then it dies.

I have only eleven weeks (or twelve) to figure this out.

HELP!

BeeAttitude for Day #91: *Blessed are those who remain calm, for they shall accomplish more.*

One thing Fran is grateful for right now: For heaven's sakes, bees, quit telling me to remain calm when I'm in a panic attack ! ! ! ! ! ! ! ! ! ! ! ! !

Forget I said that. I'm grateful for you preachy old bees, because you're usually right, doggone it.

 Day #92 Bee Suits and Police Dogs
Wednesday, Jan. 12, 2011

I tried on a beekeeper's suit a while back. The beekeeper it belonged to was a large man, at least six inches taller than my 5'7". When I got it on, all you'd have to do to make me look like the Pillsbury Doughboy was to insert lots of air. Thinking of that reminded me of a police dog I met in May of 2010.

Last year I participated in the Gwinnett County Citizens Police Academy. Two evenings a week for nine weeks. Boy, did I learn a lot.

The subject of the last class before we graduated was *the K-9 Corps.* One of the K-9 handlers came with his dog and told us about the training, the expense, the funny things that happened, and the not-so-funny. We saw some training videos and asked lots of questions.

Then the officer said, "Is there anyone who'd like to volunteer to get in the Michelin Man suit and give it a try?" My hand was the first in the air.

One thing I learned growing up was "Never Volunteer!" Trouble is, if you don't volunteer, you miss out on a lot of fun.

You also miss out on being scared enough to pee in your pants. Well, that's an exaggeration. I went potty before they zipped me into the suit. Thank goodness!

Fashion Statement

BeesKnees #1: A Beekeeping Memoir

Waiting for the command to attack

What Have I Gotten Myself Into?

I CAN'T GET UP ! ! ! !

I couldn't bend in the middle enough to stand up, so the officer grabbed the suit at my shoulder and mid-back and hauled me to my feet.

I sure am glad my bees won't be able to knock me over. I hope . . .

BeeAttitude for Day #92: *Blessed are they who are spontaneous, for they shall have good stories to tell.*

One thing Fran is grateful for right now: *Knowledgeable people who take the time to teach me.*

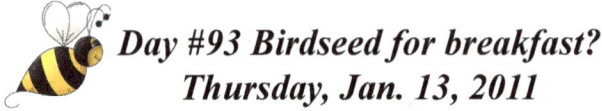 Day #93 Birdseed for breakfast? Thursday, Jan. 13, 2011

Right at the moment, which happens to be 10 a.m. on a very snowy, schools-closed, roads blocked, skylights covered, January 10th Monday morning (this is one of the blogs I wrote ahead of time in case the power goes out later today), I'm sitting at the table that nestles into my bay window watching the birds. I have lots of feeders out in the front yard, and those are mobbed this morning. I went out just after dawn and set a big tray of seed on the five or six inches of snow that fell last night, so the ground-feeders would have something to eat. As soon as I came back in the house, the first brave bird descended, checked out that unusual object, and discovered FOOD. Within moments a horde of birds fluttered around it, warming their tummies and my heart.

So, although I've never fed the birds on my back deck, not particularly wanting to encourage the leaving of bird fertilizer on the wooden planks, this morning was an exception. I swept away a swath of snow near the door, used the broom handle to write my grandchildren's names in a stretch of untouched snow, then scattered a few handfuls of seed on the bare flooring, wondering how long it would take the birds to find this new food source. By the time I walked from my back door to the bay window, they'd found it.

Cardinals, titmice, towhees, wrens, chickadees, and a few others I can't identify. Even a downy woodpecker stopped by to investigate the goings on.

Now Daisy, her whiskers twitching, is perched on the corner of the table, quivering. No wonder I don't have a TV. This is much more interesting.

Next year, if it snows again, I'll be able to look out on my deck and see the birds *and* the bees. Hmm . . .

BeeAttitude for Day #93: *Blessed are those who feed the birds, for their ears and hearts shall be filled with singing.*

One thing Fran is grateful for right now: *Wild Birds Unlimited, where I buy all my birdseed*

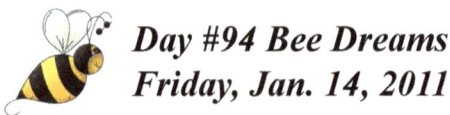

Day #94 Bee Dreams
Friday, Jan. 14, 2011

I've been dreaming about bees recently. Now don't go all Freudian on me. I think it's just that I'm spending so much of my free time (when I'm not writing or reading) with bees on my mind. Even when I knit, I think about bees. Or when I wash dishes, or any of the other myriad tasks that fill a day.

I'm getting ready to send in an order for beekeeping supplies. The smoker I already have (even though I can't figure out how to make it work), but I need a hive tool and a bee brush—yes that's what I said, a bee brush—so I can gently brush the bees away from any particular area where I need them gone. I'm also seriously thinking of buying some labels for the honey jars I hope to be able to fill. Two nights ago I dreamed that I gathered in my first honey harvest. By the end of the dream I was covered in sticky honey, with a faint coating of pollen and a fair amount of glue-like propolis all over my kitchen counter and the floor. To say nothing of the cat hair stuck in the lot. Yuck!

Oh dear. What will I do with the cats while I'm trying to cut off the honey comb?

Last night I dreamed a better dream of comb honey on breakfast biscuits, probably because I'd been talking with my sister about how wonderful comb honey is and how hard it is to find. There wasn't any cat hair in that dream, so maybe there's a way to deal with this. And maybe I'll figure it out.

BeeAttitude for Day #94: *Blessed are they who take no more than they need, for we bees shall replenish their stores.*

One thing Fran is grateful for right now: *The honey in my tea. It's not Bees Knees Honey, but next year at this time, it WILL be! I hope.*

 ### Day #95 Walking, Driving, Flying
Saturday, Jan. 15, 2011

Well, the power hasn't gone out yet, so all those posts I wrote ahead of time simply meant that, while I was sitting snug at home, unable to drive anywhere, I had more time to write. Sheer heaven for an author, to be given all that time by Mama Nature.

Five days after the Sunday night snowstorm, the Georgia schools are still closed, as are government offices and just about everything else. If we were bees, we'd just cluster together and vibrate to stay warm. But we're not bees. We need to go farther than the five-mile radius that bees fly in the summer. And we still need to get places in the winter. So, when something like this snow comes along, we're STUCK. We live in a car-centered culture, where just about everywhere we need to go is farther than walking distance. In fact, our idea of what *walking distance* is has changed drastically over the years.

I walked to school each day when I was a kid. Some years it was more than a mile. I never stepped into a school bus until I was a senior in high school, when we lived on a base that had no schools, so we Air Force brats were sent on a bus to Mascoutah, the nearest town.

Now, I live within two miles of a grocery store, but would I consider walking there and back to buy my groceries? No. And I'm within four miles of the library -- certainly a walkable distance. But again, I wouldn't dream of walking. Why? There aren't any sidewalks for more than half that distance. And no decent shoulder to walk on. I believe in walking for my health and because it feels good, but I'm not willing to put my life in danger in order to do it.

So, I guess I'll drive. As soon as I can get on the road. When ever that will be.

BeeAttitude for Day #95: *Blessed are the animals that walk and the animals that fly and even the people who drive. We bees know that how we get around isn't as important as what we do when we get there.*

One thing Fran is grateful for right now: *The skylight that finally isn't covered with snow anymore.*

Day #96 Cleaning Out My Closet
Sunday, Jan. 16, 2011

Cats wear fur, bees wear fuzz and wings, people wear—well, as far as I can see it, we have way too many choices. A dozen or so years ago I visited a long-lost cousin in Tennessee, and she showed me through her house. Her closet was the size of my living room. I felt completely overwhelmed. My clothes closet was half the size of her linen closet. How can anyone ever choose when there are so many possibilities available?

Still, even with relatively few choices, I've found that sometimes I put an outfit on, only to sigh and replace it with one I'm more comfortable in. I read once that we wear 20% of our wardrobe 80% of the time. I think that's right. Last week, when I was talking with my Master Mind partner, I decided that I would delete a quarter of the clothes in my closet—all the ones I don't like wearing anyway.

I went through my closet and pulled out everything that I didn't absolutely love to wear. Loaded it all in the back seat of my car to take to Goodwill. And there it still sits, since the ice is so bad I can't get to Goodwill. Or anywhere else.

Things will melt eventually, and in the meantime, my closet has in it only what I will wear with joy.

Of course, this whole past week I've been wearing nothing but sweats. When one is snowed in, it doesn't make sense to dress up.

A quarter of my cousin's closet would fill a small U-Haul. Have you cleaned out your closet lately?

BeeAttitude for Day #96: *Blessed are those who live simply, for they shall not be confused.*

One thing Fran is grateful for right now: *All the room I have.*

# Day #97 January Building Project
Monday, Jan. 17, 2011

I just realized it's January.

Dumb, huh? Of *course* it's January. But January in a normal (i.e. pre-bee) year was just a time to gather my momentum for the coming year.

This time, it's *Uh-oh! Only about 9 weeks left!* And I was planning to build a top-bar hive to put my package of bees in.

I have some plans I bought from www.BeeLanding.com. Now, all I need is:

- lots of wood
- a bunch of wood-screws
- two hinges
- a rectangle of glass (so I can make a viewing port)
- some steel thingies to brace the angles

I'd better visit Home Depot tomorrow.

I could also use a friend with a table saw. Know where I can get one of those?

BeeAttitude for Day #97: *Blessed are those who plan ahead, for we shall settle happily into our new home and produce great stores of honey for them.*

One thing Fran is grateful for right now: *My wonderful sister who, I hope, is having a delightful birthday*

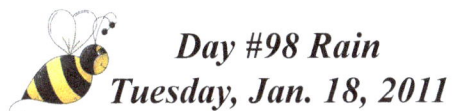 Day #98 Rain
Tuesday, Jan. 18, 2011

Well, first it snowed, and now it's raining, and I'm wondering how bees get by in a downpour.

I'm pretty sure a lot of bees don't make it back to the hive when it rains, since they can't fly with wet wings. Imagine how much a drop of water must weigh compared to a whisper-light bee wing. And they'd probably get pretty cold without their sisters to cluster with.

Boy, do I take my roof and my furnace for granted!

BeeAttitude for Day #98: *Blessed are those who build hive bodies for us, for they shall sleep well, knowing they are saving us bees.*

One thing Fran is grateful for right now: *Cool-Ray Heating and Air, the folks who put in my good furnace.*

Day #99 Ninety-nine? Hooray!
Wednesday, Jan. 19, 2011

When I started this 600-day project more than three months ago, I wasn't 100% sure I'd be able to keep it up. So today, I'm going to celebrate a bit. Let's see . . . how should I do this?

- Eat chocolate
- Read another bee book chapter or two
- Write another blog entry
- Pat a cat or two
- Order the rest of the beekeeping supplies I'll need next March
- All of the above

What do you want to bet the last one wins?

BeeAttitude for Day #99: *Blessed are those who persevere, for they shall accomplish much.*

One thing Fran is grateful for right now: *Warm homemade bread drizzled with real butter*

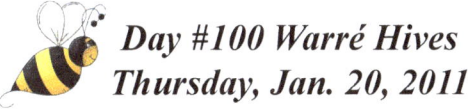 Day #100 Warré Hives
Thursday, Jan. 20, 2011

Warré (pronounced war-ray) hives look like regular old beehives, except that they are top-bar hives (which means the bees build the cells all by themselves, rather than starting out with pre-formed plastic—*i.e. human-made*—sheets of foundation). I just found out about Warré hives on the internet, and I even downloaded the plans—39 pages that assume one has a table saw. Doggone it!

TheBeeSpace.net

Now, I figure that bees have been building hives for 140 million years utilizing whatever old hollow trees they could find. So, instead of freaking out about needing a $$$$$$ table $aw $$$$$$$, I'm going to build some 4-sided boxes without tops or bottoms, throw in some bars across the top of each box, build a roof, and see what the bees do with the result. I'd better use screws instead of nails, so they don't fall apart.

Yeah, I know, I have to be really specific about the distance between the bars if I ever want to steal—er—harvest honey. I can do that. Of course, with the way I build, those boxes are liable to look a bit lopsided. But, hey, they're going on my back deck, and I can't imagine the bees will give a hoot anyway.

BeeAttitude for Day #100: *Blessed are those who do the best they can with what they have, for they shall never be uptight.*

One thing Fran is grateful for right now: *My dad, who taught me how to swing a hammer*

[You can continue the BeesKnees Beekeeping journey in volumes two through six.]

www.ingramcontent.com/pod-product-compliance
Lightning Source LLC
Chambersburg PA
CBHW071712020426
42333CB00017B/2230